Scroll Saw
for the first time®

OPHELIA'S WORLD
Michele Durkson Clise
Potter
THE VELVETEEN RABBIT
WILLIAMS/ATKINSON
KNOPF
YOU ARE SPECIAL
MAX LUCADO
Burnett
Sunflower Houses
Lovejoy
HOLLYHOCK DAYS
ALFONS MUCHA
DRUSE

Scroll Saw
for the first time®

Dirk Boelman

STERLING/CHAPELLE
An imprint of Sterling Publishing Co., Inc.

New York / London
www.sterlingpublishing.com

Chapelle, Ltd.:
Jo Packham
Sara Toliver
Cindy Stoeckl

Editor: Ray Cornia
Art Director: Karla Haberstich
Copy Editor: Marilyn Goff
Photographers: Ryne Hazen and Kevin Dilley for Hazen Photography
Photo Stylists: Connie Duran and Suzy Skadburg
Graphic Illustrator: Kim Taylor

Staff: Kelly Ashkettle, Areta Bingham, Anne Bruns, Donna Chambers, Emily Frandsen, Lana Hall, Susan Jorgensen, Jennifer Luman, Melissa Maynard, Barbara Milburn, Lecia Monsen, Linda Venditti, Desirée Wybrow

If you have any questions or comments, please contact:
Chapelle, Ltd., Inc., P.O. Box 9252, Ogden, UT 84409
(801) 621-2777 • (801) 621-2788 Fax
e-mail: chapelle@chapelleltd.com
web sites: www.chapelleltd.com
www.rubyandbegonia.com

Library of Congress Cataloging-in-Publication Data available

10 9 8 7 6 5 4 3 2 1

Published by Sterling Publishing Co., Inc.
387 Park Avenue South, New York, NY 10016
©2004 by Dirk Boelman
Distributed in Canada by Sterling Publishing
c/o Canadian Manda Group, 165 Dufferin Street
Toronto, Ontario, Canada M6K 3H6
Distributed in the United Kingdom by GMC Distribution Services
Castle Place, 166 High Street, Lewes, East Sussex, England BN7 1XU
Distributed in Australia by Capricorn Link (Australia) Pty. Ltd.
P.O. Box 704, Windsor, NSW 2756, Australia
Printed and Bound in China
All Rights Reserved

Sterling   ISBN 13: 978-1-4027-0817-6 Hardback
ISBN 10: 1-4027-0817-3
ISBN 13: 978-1-4027-5183-7 Paperback
ISBN 10: 1-4027-5183-4

For information about custom editions, special sales, premium and corporate purchases, please contact Sterling Special Sales Department at 800-805-5489 or specialsales@sterlingpub.com.

Table of Contents

Section 4:
New Dimensions in Scroll
Sawing—82

Introduction

A brief history

Scroll sawing is a centuries-old form of decorative and ornamental woodworking. It has evolved from being created with hand-held saws, to foot-powered treadle and pedal saws, to the electric-motor-driven, multispeed, multifeatured precision scroll-saw machines of today.

The art of cutting intricate twists and turns, and cutouts in wood, has been used to produce everything from clocks, shelves, frames, and furniture, to toys, games, and puzzles, as well as architectural trim work and embellishments.

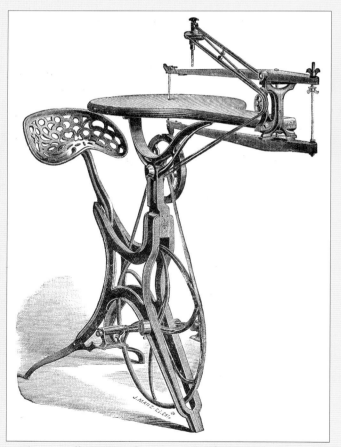

Above, an illustration from an early mail-order catalogue shows the type of equipment used when scroll-sawing first became popular in the United States.

Its roots can be traced to early Oriental, Scandinavian, German, and Italian designs, reaching a peak in America during the Victorian era. In the 1930s and 1950s it lost some of its glory as Americans became intrigued with the straight lines of the Arts and Crafts movement, Frank Lloyd Wright's Prairie Style architecture, and designs influenced by Stickley and Mission Style furnishings. However, there has been a huge resurgence in interest in scroll sawing, which began in the 1980s with the development of new and improved scroll saws, and it continues to capture the interests of people of all ages and skill levels.

Although much of the history about scroll sawing, as well as patterns and finished projects, was lost during World Wars I and II, some of the old patterns and catalogs survived. Thanks to a few people who maintained an interest in scroll sawing, or fretwork (as it was referred to years ago), in spite of world events and changes in popular opinions regarding style and design, scroll sawing is very much alive and well today.

Today

Scroll sawing has grown to become one of the most popular of the contemporary craft hobbies. It is one of the safest of all forms of woodworking, requiring a minimal amount of space, tools, and materials. It is a hobby that grows with you as you tackle an ever-growing array of tempting and challenging projects.

How to Use This Book

Remember, we all start out at the same point, as beginners, newcomers to the art of scroll sawing. You need no special skills or talents; however, a very basic understanding of woodworking and woodworking tools is necessary. The most important requirements are the ability to learn to follow a pattern line using a scroll saw and the desire to create something beautiful with your own hands. Don't let yourself become frustrated if things don't turn out "perfectly" the first time. My goal with this book is to give you a quick introduction into the basics of scroll sawing; turn you loose on a variety of projects that get progressively more difficult; and show you that there's no better way to learn than from experience. The more sawing you do, the better you will become at it.

This book has been divided into four sections. Each section builds upon the skills learned in the previous segment.

Section 1: Scroll Saw Basics

This section provides you with almost everything you need to know about basic scroll sawing. You will make a few practice cuts to become familiar and comfortable with how the scroll saw works—to get a "feel" for feeding the wood into the saw blade and what it's like to try to get the blade to follow the line. Don't get frustrated or discouraged—practice makes perfect.

Section 2: Basic Scroll Saw Techniques

Here you will use the basic techniques to make a series of projects, learn about selecting materials, follow instructions, etc. Each project will build upon the skills learned from the previous projects, as you gain experience at manipulating the blade to follow the pattern lines.

Section 3: Beyond the Basics

At the beginning of this section, you are provided with information to help you advance further into your new hobby: assembling a handy tool kit to keep by your saw, and tips and techniques to help as you begin to tackle more elaborate/complex projects. A series of projects will challenge you to try other scroll-sawing techniques.

Section 4: New Dimensions for Scroll Sawing

This section will show you how to go beyond flat projects. Here you will tackle projects that are three-dimensional, learn to cut other materials, and try a few other slightly more difficult projects as you explore the versatility of the scroll saw.

Above, author Dirk Boelman, is an acknowledged scroll saw expert. He is often asked to evaluate scroll saw equipment.

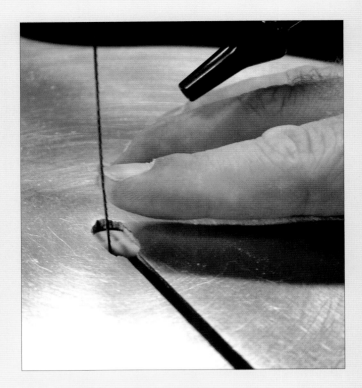

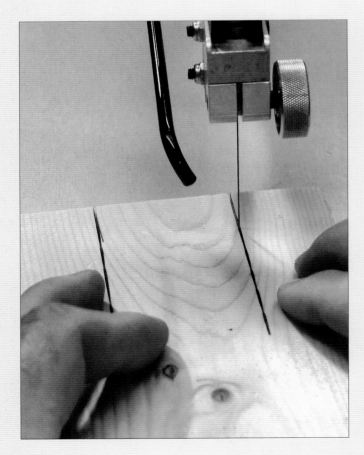

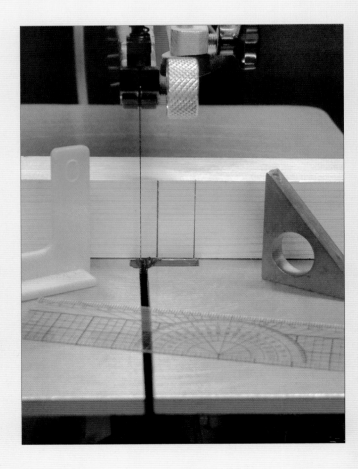

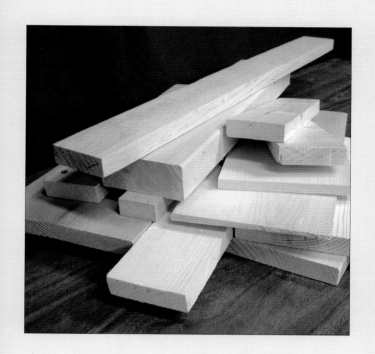

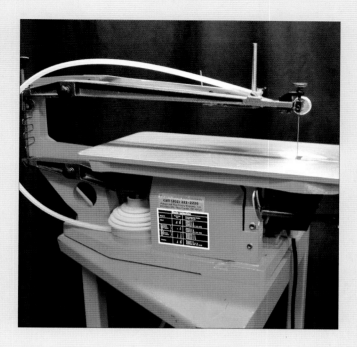

Section 1: Scroll Saw Basics

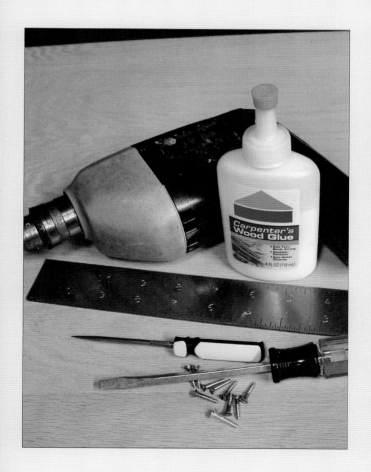

How to get started?

To begin, you will need a scroll saw (along with any tools and accessories needed to operate your saw), a few scroll-saw blades, and some wood.

The scroll saw

There are many models and sizes of scroll saws available from a host of manufacturers (see pictures below). Each machine will have its own specifications and special features. Among the features you should look for when shopping for a scroll saw are: variable speeds, pinless (plain end) blade holders that are quick and easy to open and close, and quick-and-easy tension-setting devices.

Above, there are many brands and styles of scroll saws available.

Setting up your scroll saw

Take time to properly set up your machine. Saws with stands usually employ some method of adjusting the legs or feet to balance or level it on uneven floors. Making these adjustments will ensure that your saw will operate smoothly, with less vibration and noise. Likewise, securely fasten benchtop saws to the bench or tabletop with bolts or clamps. In all instances, refer to the manufacturer's instructions to aid with set up.

Next, make certain your saw table is adjusted perpendicular, or square, with the blade. You can check by using a small square, angle gauge, or protractor. Another method is to use a carpenter's square to draw a line, in red ink, on a block of wood (see picture below). Place the block behind the blade, and adjust the saw table as needed to line up the blade perfectly with the red line.

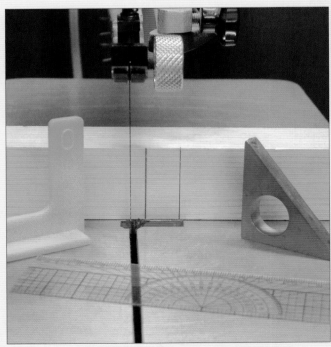

Above, various tools may be used to check the angle of the blade in relation to the table.

In addition, make certain you have adequate lighting available that does not create a shadow near the blade. Such a shadow makes it difficult to see where you are sawing. You may want a comfortable stool or chair so you can sit down while sawing. Before going any further—read the safety and operating instructions provided with your machine!

Safety

The hobby of scroll sawing is a safe and enjoyable activity provided all safety rules are obeyed. To disregard prudent safety considerations invites injury. Please remember the following safety guidelines:

• Understand and follow manufacturers' instructions regarding the safe operation of all tools and materials.

• Keep fingers away from moving blades or cutting instruments. Use the eraser end of a pencil as a "push stick" to hold down and maneuver the wood when in the process of cutting, the blade comes too close to your fingers.

• Use ear and eye protection when working with power tools. It is a good idea to use eye protection at all times.

• Wear a dust mask or respirator while working.

• Wear proper attire, remove jewelry and loose clothing, and secure long hair. Wear shoes that will offer protection from falling or sharp objects.

• Keep your mind on your work. If you can't stay focused on the work, put it away for another day. It is not worth an accident to finish a woodworking project one day earlier.

• Use common sense at all times.

Basic tools and supplies

As you begin working with the scroll saw, you are going to need a few simple tools and supplies:

• #4 x ⅝" flat-head wood screws
• Awl
• Cardboard box
• Clean rags
• Masking tape
• Medium-sized standard screwdriver
• Paintbrushes in assorted sizes
• Power drill and drill bits
• Ruler
• Sandpaper, 80- to 400-grit
• Scissors
• Small carpenter's square
• Soft-lead pencil
• Spray adhesive
• Wood finishes, canola oil, acrylic paints, and natural Danish oil finish
• Wood glue

Above, a power drill, wood glue, a small carpenter's square, an awl, wood screws, and a screwdriver are basic tools and materials used when making scroll-saw projects.

Blades

There are many sizes and styles of blades available from the various manufacturers. To keep things simple, we will start out using just two styles of blades in this book—skip tooth and reverse tooth (see illustration 1a below).

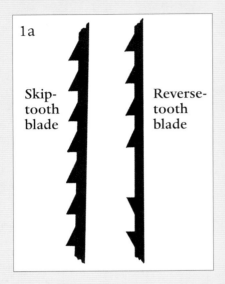

1a

Skip-tooth blade

Reverse-tooth blade

Skip-tooth blades are the "basic" scroll saw blades. So named because there is a space, or "skip," between each tooth. They are available in a wide range of sizes, which are numbered from small to large, e.g. 3/0, 2/0, 2, 4.

Reverse-tooth blades are manufactured with a few teeth pointing in the opposite direction at the bottom of the blade. These teeth are designed to cut on the "up-stroke" of the scroll saw, to reduce and clean up the amount of tear-out, or fuzz, that often occurs on the bottom of the workpiece as the blade exits the wood on the down stroke with regular-toothed blades.

Other blade styles include double tooth, spiral, crown tooth, precision ground, metal cutting, glass cutting, and jeweler's blades. You may choose to experiment with various types of blades as you

expand your interests in scroll sawing; but for now, all you need is a dozen each of #0, #2, #5, and #7 skip-tooth blades, and a dozen each of #2, #5, and #7 reverse-tooth blades.

As you begin to use your scroll saw, you will notice the left side of the blade produces a smoother edge because there is a slight burr on the right side of the blade (see illustration 1b below). The burr or rough edge is produced when the blade is manufactured and machines press or stamp them out.

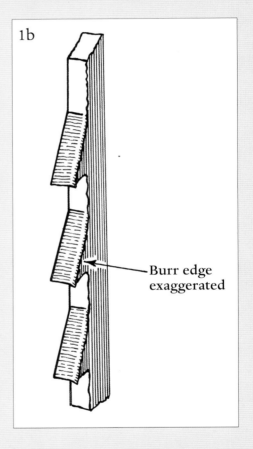

1b

Burr edge exaggerated

Also, because of the burr on the right side of the blade, this side cuts through the material a little faster than the smooth left side. For this reason you need to compensate slightly as you feed the wood into the blade. For example, draw a straight line on a piece of wood. If you push it exactly straight into the front teeth of the blade you will see the blade start to cut toward the right side of the line (see picture below).

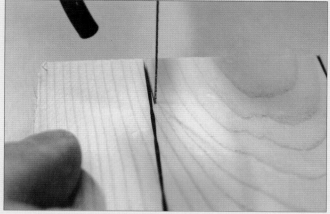

Above, blades naturally "pull" to the right when feeding the wood directly into the blade.

To correct for the action of the blade, angle the wood slightly to the right as you feed it into the blade. You will find it is much easier to follow a line (see picture below).

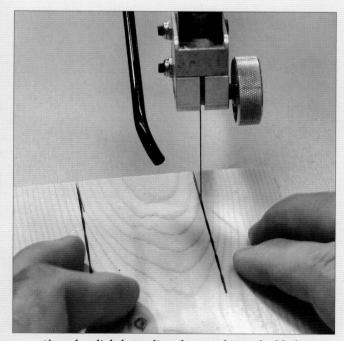

Above, by slightly angling the wood into the blade, it is easier to make the blade follow the line.

To see the difference between skip-tooth versus reverse-tooth blades, install a #7 skip-tooth blade in your scroll saw. Make a cut with this blade. Next, install a #7 reverse-tooth blade in the scroll saw, and repeat the cut.

Compare the bottom edges of the wood, and see how differently the two saw blades cut (see pictures below).

Above, detail of the bottom side of wood cut with a skip-tooth blade.

Above, detail of the bottom side of wood cut with a reverse-tooth blade.

Keep in mind that "all blades are not created equal." Some are manufactured differently, some are made from one type of metal, and some are made from another. Some work better on a particular brand of scroll saw. Some woodworkers cut fast and some go slowly. Since scroll-saw blades are quite inexpensive, try different ones. Eventually you will find the right blades for you.

Wood

There is a huge selection of solid woods and ply-woods available (see picture below). You will learn about using some of them as you tackle various projects in this book. To start out, all you need are a few scrap pieces of pine. It is relatively inexpensive, easy to find, and easy to work with. It is considered to be a softwood, making it fairly easy to cut and perfect to use when you are just starting out.

Above, wood comes in many sizes and thicknesses.

You will need to start locating sources for various thicknesses and species of solid woods, and ply-woods. Check your local area for lumber yards, home improvement stores, and specialty wood out-lets. As you visit these various stores, look for a wood expert who can answer questions about various woods and their unique properties.

We will expand upon this "basic list" of tools and materials as we work our way through the book. For now, let's saw!

Scroll-sawing techniques

Step 1: Install a #7 skip-tooth blade in your scroll saw, following the manufacturer's instructions. Fasten the top and bottom blade holders, and apply tension on the blade. If your scroll-saw instructions do not recommend a manner in which to determine how much tension should be put on the blade, tighten it until it produces a high-pitched "twang" when plucked like a guitar string. Most often there is a tendency to put too little tension on a blade. There is too little tension if it can be easily pushed to the side (see picture below). There may be too much tension if you break several blades in a short period of time, or find it difficult to keep the blades fastened in the blade holders while sawing.

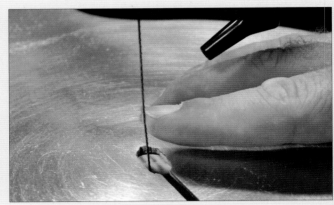
Above, blade should not easily bend when touched.

Step 2: Place a scrap piece of ½"- or ¾"-thick wood, roughly 4" square, on the saw table. With your saw running at a slow-to-medium speed, cut off one of the corners (see picture below). You may notice that the blade has a tendency to "lift" the wood. Because of this tendency, maintain a steady downward pressure on the top of the wood to prevent it from being lifted and then slammed back down again on the saw table. Notice the hand positions in relation to the blade. The scroll saw is one of the safest wood-working tools; but

Above, cutting corner of wood.

do not get your fingers too close to the blade, or between other moving parts where they may become pinched or injured.

Step 3: Next, saw through the wood as you swing it gently to the left and right to create a wavy cut (see picture below). Again be aware of the tendency for the wood to be lifted. Also notice the amount of effort needed to push the wood into the saw blade. Continue "slicing" off pieces of wood as you get a feel for the speed at which you can push or "feed" the wood into the blade without it seeming like you are rushing the process, or causing the saw blade to work extra hard to cut through the material. This "feed rate" needs to be the speed at which the blade "cruises" through the wood without bending the blade backward. Take your time, make plenty of practice cuts, and get comfortable with the basic operation of the scroll saw.

Above, practice cutting a wavy line with the saw.

Step 4: Now it is time to start learning how to maneuver the wood, and the blade, to get the scroll saw to follow a line. Draw some irregular lines on a piece of scrap wood. Try to saw through the wood, following your drawn lines. Take your time and saw directly on the line. It takes a bit of practice, so repeat the process until you feel comfortable with it.

Step 5: Practice making very sharp inside and outside corner cuts. Take a piece of wood and either draw a design (see illustration 1c below), or glue a copy of the design onto the wood.

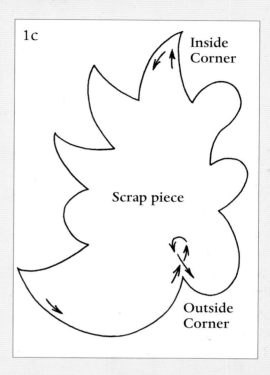

For this exercise, imagine the interior shape as the waste area. When you come to an outside corner, loop into the waste area and come back to the line to make a sharp corner (see picture below).

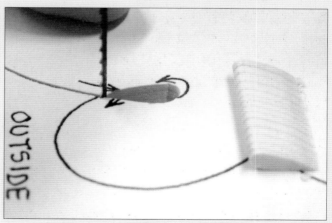

Above, looping beyond an outside corner creates a very sharp corner or tip.

To make a sharp inside corner, cut into the corner (see picture below). Stop at the corner and then back the blade about ⅜" in the saw cut. Pivot the wood 180° so the teeth on the blade cut into the waste side of the wood.

Above, bring blade right to the inside corner and stop. Back the blade up a short distance (approximately ⅜").

Back the blade down the saw cut and into the corner (see picture below). From the corner, cut your way out the other side of the corner and continue cutting in a counterclockwise direction.

Above, notice the small round hole behind the top arrow. This is where the blade was turned.

Draw or glue the design onto another piece of wood and repeat the cutting process, except make the outside shape the scrap piece.

Repeat these exercises with wood of various thicknesses and with different sizes of saw blades. It will not take long before you can follow any pattern.

Project finishing

This is a subject where there are many strong opinions. Since this book is about learning to scroll saw, only a very basic treatment of finishing and finishing techniques will be offered.

After an object is cut with the scroll saw, it should be sanded before any finish is applied. Sandpaper comes in many "grits" or degrees of roughness. A course-grit sandpaper should be used first (60- to 100-grit). This type of sandpaper is to smooth out the imperfections made by the saw.

Once the wood is smooth, medium-grit sandpaper (150- to 200-grit) is used to polish the wood. This type of sandpaper is for making all areas of the wood universally smooth and polished. Some woodworkers will not go beyond this sanding for many of their projects.

If a high-gloss finish is desired, a fine-grit sandpaper may be used (250- to 400-grit). The wood will become shiny and ultrasmooth when sanded with this type of sandpaper. Use a clean cloth to wipe away dust caused by sanding.

Above, a course-grit sandpaper is used first as pictured here on the bottom of the stack. A medium-grit is used next to smooth the wood. Lastly, a fine-grit sandpaper is used to put a polish finish on the wood.

Above, there are many products for coloring or protecting wood. Some are made for easy application while others give a durable finish. Always test finishes on scrap material before applying to a project.

Once the object is sanded, a protective finish should be applied. One of the simplest finishes to apply is canola oil. Canola oil is a safe and nontoxic finish for projects that might be handled by small children. It is applied with a rag, allowed to dry for a few minutes, and then excess oil is wiped away with a clean cloth.

Stain can be applied to give the wood more color. It can be applied with a rag, a foam brush, or a regular paintbrush. Stains come in water-based and oil-based varieties. As expected, the water-based stains clean up easier. Stains do not usually seal the wood, so many woodworkers cover a stain with varnish.

Some projects in this book need to be painted. I prefer to use acrylic paint because it is less toxic than many other types of paint and it is easy to clean up. Acrylic paint can be sprayed on or applied with a brush. It can be applied directly to the wood, but it lasts longer if a primer coat is applied first.

Whether you choose to stain, oil finish, or paint your project, follow the instructions for use provided by the manufacturer of the product. Proper application, storage, and disposal of these products is important to the successful completion of your woodworking projects and the overall safety to yourself and your family.

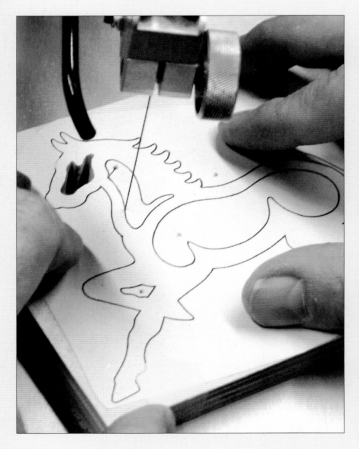

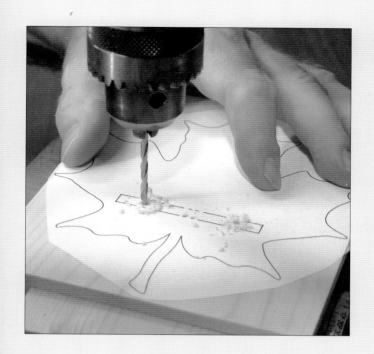

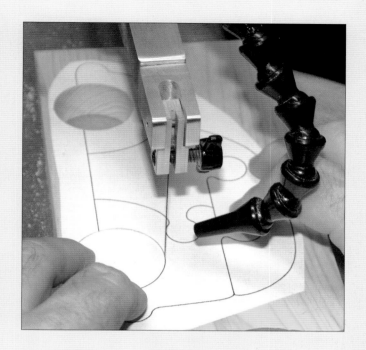

Section 2: Basic Scroll Saw Techniques

1
Technique

How do I attach a pattern onto the wood and then cut a basic shape?

Spray adhesive works great to temporarily attach a pattern to the wood surface. Using a pattern as a guide for cutting is the magic of scroll-sawing. Patterns enable you to make almost any project.

Simple Fish

Here's how:

1. Select a clear piece of pine.

2. Photocopy the Simple Fish Pattern below. The pattern can also be enlarged or reduced for future use.

*What you need
to get started:*

Tools:
- Basic tools and supplies page 13
- Photocopier
- Scroll saw with #7 skip-tooth blade
- Power drill with ³⁄₁₆" bit

Materials:
- Pine board ¾" x 3½" x 5"
- Canola oil

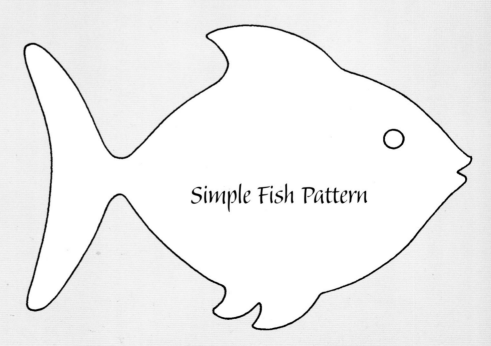

Simple Fish Pattern

Continued on page 24

Above, finished project size: ¾" x 4¾" x 3¼". Canola oil finish.

Continued from page 22

3. Use scissors to trim away excess paper around pattern.

4. Use inverted cardboard box as a spray booth. Place pattern face down in box. Spray light coating of glue onto back of pattern (see picture below). Allow glue to get "tacky," this takes about six seconds.

5. Temporarily adhere pattern onto wood by firmly rubbing it down with fingertips.
   NOTES: Pattern would be permanently attached if spray adhesive were to be applied to both pattern and wood.
   Wondering which way the wood grain should be on your scroll saw projects? Most of the time the grain should run in the same direction as the longest dimension of your project.

6. Install #7 skip-tooth blade on scroll saw. Place wood on saw and cut along pattern lines. (Refer to Scroll-sawing Techniques, Step 5 on pages 17–18.)
   NOTE: Cut in clockwise direction to keep waste material on right-hand side of blade.

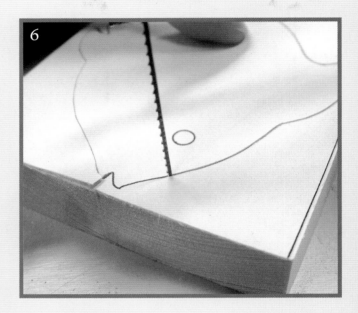

7. Use awl to mark center point within eye.

8. Using ³⁄₁₆" bit, drill perpendicular hole through awl mark in eye.

9. Remove pattern from wood and sand smooth with sandpaper. Start with 80-grit and finish with 200- to 400-grit. (Refer to Project Finishing on page 18.)
   NOTE: After you have cut out a project and removed the pattern no one will ever know if you have wandered off the line a little bit.

10. Using rag, apply canola oil as a finish. Allow canola oil to dry for a few minutes, then wipe excess oil off with a clean rag. (Refer to Project Finishing on page 19.)

How do I cut out a shape within the body of the wood?

A hole must be drilled within the body of the wood. Then the saw blade is inserted into the hole and reconnected to the scroll saw. After cutting out the shape, disconnect the blade and remove.

Scotty Dog and Lucky Cat

Here's how:

1. Photocopy the Scotty Dog and Lucky Cat Patterns on page 28.

2. Temporarily adhere pattern onto wood with spray adhesive. (Refer to Simple Fish, Steps 3–5 on page 24.)
    NOTE: If wood has a straight, machined edge, position pattern with paws directly on edge (see picture below). This ensures that figurines will stand straight.

2
Technique

What you need to get started:

Tools:
- Basic tools and supplies page 13
- Photocopier
- Power drill with ⅟₁₆" bit
- Scroll saw with #7 reverse-tooth blade

Materials:
- Two pieces of pine board ¾" x 5¼" x 6½"
- Black acrylic paint
- Ribbons, bows, small bell

Above, finished project size: ¾" x 6" x 5". Black acrylic paint finish.

3. Use awl to mark center point within eye.

4. Using ¹⁄₁₆" bit, drill perpendicular hole through awl mark in eye (see picture below).

5. Install #7 reverse-tooth blade in scroll saw. Thread blade through eye hole (see picture below). Fasten blade in scroll saw and carefully cut out eye. (Refer to Scroll-sawing Techniques, Step 5 on pages 17–18.)

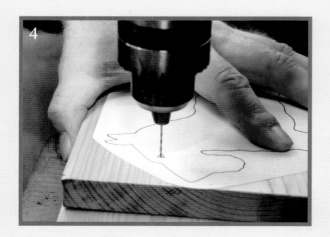

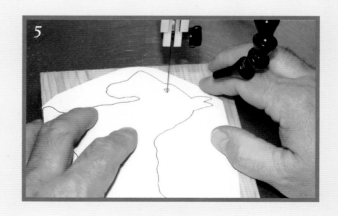

6. Remove blade from eye opening. Refasten blade in scroll saw and cut around outer profile in clockwise direction to finish cutting out project.

7. Remove pattern from wood and use coarse sandpaper to touch-up any imperfections on figurine. Also, remove fuzz on back side, and soften sharp edges. Finish sanding all surfaces to desired smoothness. (Refer to Project Finishing on page 18.)

8. Remove all dust with clean rag, and apply black acrylic paint with paintbrush. (Refer to Project Finishing on page 19.)

NOTES: Experiment with paint on scrap material before applying to project. Always carefully follow manufacturer's directions for paint application, storage and disposal.

Figurines in upper photograph on page 26 are painted with black acrylic paint, thinned with water. The set pictured below is finished with a coat of canola oil.

9. Add decorative ribbons and bows, and a jingling bell for the Lucky Cat. These decorative touches should match the decor where figurines will be displayed, or they can reflect a holiday motif and change with the season.

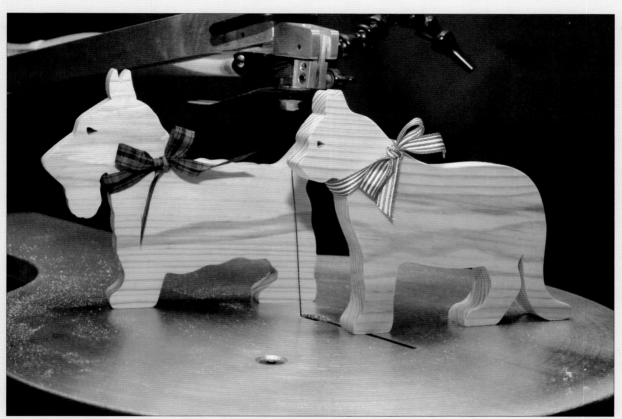

Above, Scotty Dog and Lucky Cat shown with canola oil finish.

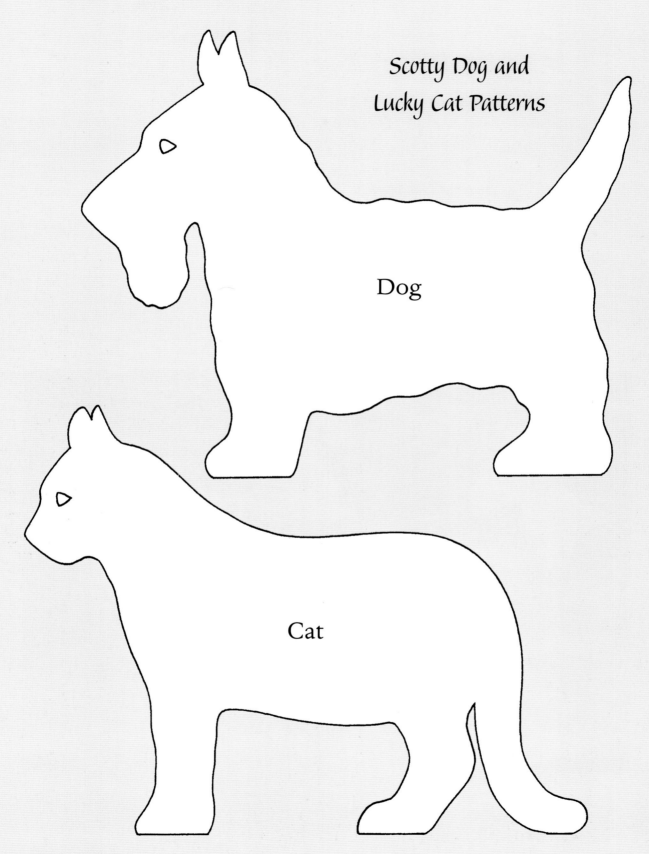

Scotty Dog and
Lucky Cat Patterns

Dog

Cat

How do I make a simple jigsaw puzzle?

A puzzle can be made by cutting out a simple shape and then cutting that shape into puzzle pieces. By painting the puzzle pieces with bright colors, a charming jigsaw puzzle is created.

Putt-putt Puzzles

Here's how:

1. Photocopy the Putt-putt Puzzles Patterns on page 32.

2. Temporarily adhere patterns onto wood with spray adhesive. (Refer to Simple Fish, Steps 3–5 on page 24.)

3. Install #5 reverse-tooth blade in scroll saw. Begin by carefully following the pattern lines to cut out round wheels (see picture below).
   NOTE: Small blades cut sharp curves, twists, and turns. Because they are so thin, the saw cut (or kerf) is very narrow, allowing the puzzle pieces to fit together and interlock.

3
Technique

What you need to get started:

Tools:
- Basic tools and supplies page 13
- Photocopier
- Scroll saw with #5 reverse-tooth blade

Materials:
- ¾" x 3¼" x 6¾" clear pine board
- ¾" x 4" x 7¼" clear pine board
- Acrylic paints in black, blue, orange, red, and yellow

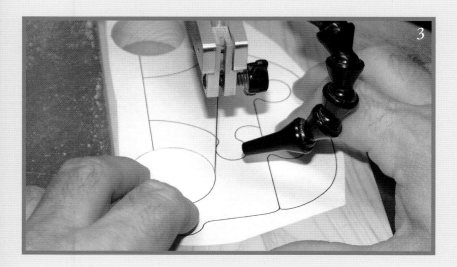

Above, finished project size: 1" x 7" x 3¾ ". Acrylic paint finish.

4. Cut around outer profile (see picture below).

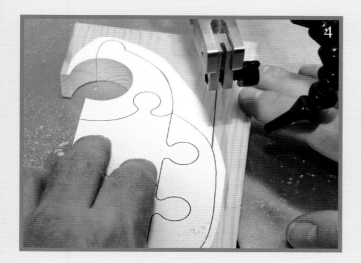

5. Separate the pieces of puzzle by cutting away sections in the following order: first, cut off roof/top section (see picture below), then, cut apart three sections of body.

NOTE: Do not push or crowd wood into the blade. You do not want to force the blade to the left or right, nor to the back or front. Keep the blade cutting through the wood perfectly straight up and down. This ensures the puzzle pieces can be easily separated and reassembled.

6. After cutting all pieces, remove patterns (see picture below). Touch up imperfections and soften any sharp edges with sandpaper. Finish sanding all surfaces to desired smoothness. (Refer to Project Finishing on page 18.)

7. Apply colorful acrylic finish by thinning acrylic paints with water and smoothly brushing onto wood, following the grain of the wood. Allow one side of the puzzle to completely dry before painting the other side. Puzzle will probably require several coats because wood will absorb a great deal of the paint. (Refer to Project Finishing on page 19.)

NOTES: Paint adds thickness to wood, so keep paint thin on sides of puzzle that fit together.

Remember that projects meant for children should always use safe nontoxic finishes.

Putt-putt Puzzles Patterns

How do I properly attach a shelf onto a decorative scroll–saw design?

Careful measurement will allow you to drill pilot holes so screws can be inserted into the shelf for an invisible yet strong bond.

Maple Leaf Shelf

Here's how:

1. Photocopy Maple Leaf Shelf Patterns on page 37. Use scissors to trim away excess paper around pattern. Position pattern for shelf onto wood to take advantage of a straight edge (see picture below). Temporarily adhere patterns onto wood with spray adhesive. (Refer to Simple Fish, Steps 4–5 on page 24.)

What you need to get started:

Tools:
- Basic tools and supplies page 13
- Photocopier
- Scroll saw with #5 reverse-tooth blade
- Power drill with $\frac{5}{32}$", $\frac{1}{8}$", and countersink bits
- Foam brush

Materials:
- $\frac{1}{4}$" x $5\frac{1}{4}$" x $8\frac{1}{2}$" clear pine board
- (2) #4 x $\frac{5}{8}$" flat-head wood screws

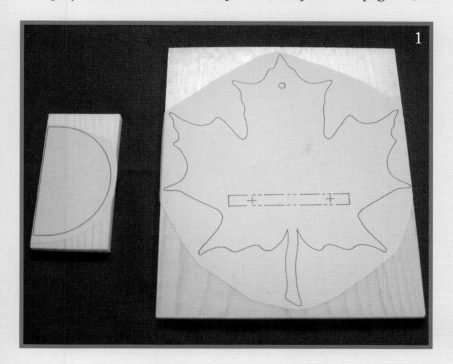

Above, finished project size: ¼" x 5⅛" x 5⅞". Natural Danish oil finish.

2. Install #5 reverse-tooth blade in scroll saw. Cut out shelf and maple leaf. (Refer to Scroll-sawing Techniques, Step 5 on pages 17–18.)

3. Before removing pattern from leaf back, use awl to mark center point for the hanging hole at the top, and for two mounting screws that attach shelf (see picture below).

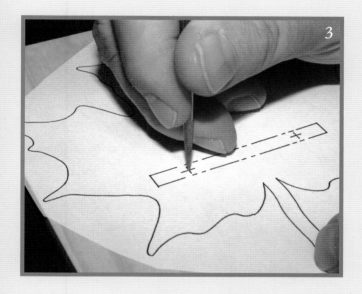

4. Use awl marks as guides to drill ⁵⁄₃₂" hanging hole, and two ⅛" shelf-mounting holes (see picture below).

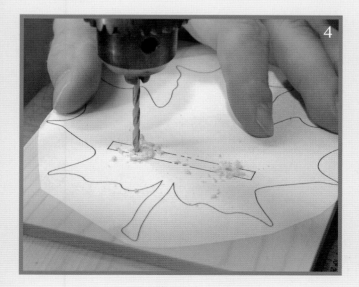

5. On leaf back, use countersink bit so screw heads can be set flush with surface of the wood when installing shelf (see picture below).

6. Remove patterns from wood. Touch up any imperfections with sandpaper. Finish sanding to desired smoothness. (Refer to Project Finishing on page 18.)

7. Lay shelf flat on leaf back, centered left to right, with edge approximately halfway over the mounting-screw holes. Use pencil to carefully mark centers, for pilot holes, on shelf edge (see picture below).

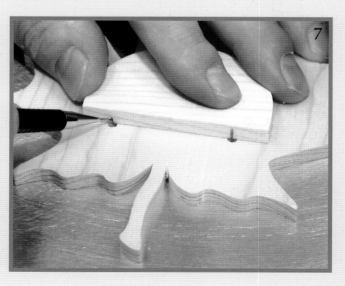

8. Use ruler to measure to the center of the thickness of shelf. Mark center points for pilot holes (see picture below). Use awl to mark locations, then drill ¹⁄₁₆" holes approximately ¼" deep into edge of shelf.

9. Test-fit shelf to leaf by temporarily installing mounting screws. Align shelf perpendicular to leaf back piece.
   NOTES: A small block of wood can be used as guide/jig to aid with shelf assembly (see picture below).
   If shelf does not attach perfectly, you can use sandpaper to adjust rear edge of shelf to eliminate any upward or downward slant.

10. When satisfied with shelf attachment, apply a small amount of wood glue on back of shelf, and secure to leaf with screws. Wipe away excess glue.

11. When glue is dry, remove all dust with a dry rag, and apply natural Danish oil finish. Danish oil can be applied using a foam brush or a rag. After it has dried for a few minutes, wipe away excess oil. (Refer to Project Finishing on page 19.)
    NOTE: If you would like to have a little larger shelf, simply enlarge the patterns on a photocopier and use thicker wood.

Above, Maple Leaf Shelf can also be painted in brilliant fall colors to celebrate the season.

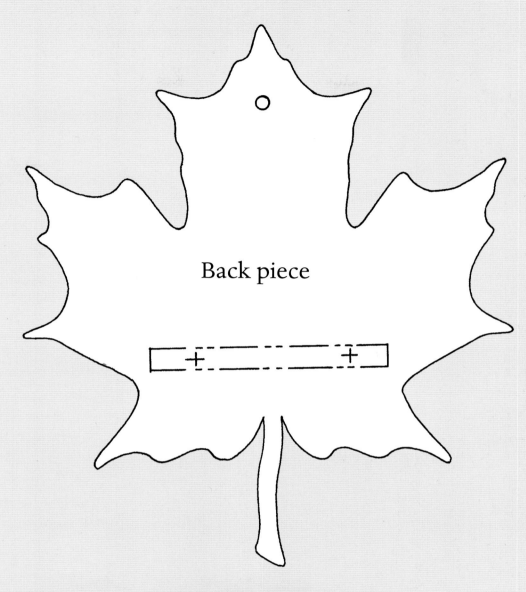

Back piece

Maple Leaf Shelf Patterns

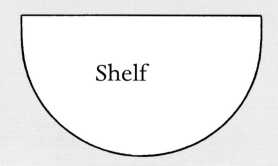

Shelf

5
Technique

What you need to get started:

Tools:
- Basic tools and supplies page 13
- Photocopier
- Scroll saw with #5 reverse-tooth blade
- Drill with ¹⁄₁₆" bit
- Needle files

Materials:
- (2) Horse ⅛" x 4¼" x 5½" baltic birch plywood
- (2) Heart angel ⅛" x 3½" x 5¼" baltic birch plywood
- (2) Praying angel ⅛" x 3¼" x 5¼" baltic birch plywood
- White acrylic spray paint
- Colored ribbons and beads

How do I make multiple copies of the same project all at one time?

"Stack sawing" is a technique that allows you to make several identical scroll-saw items all at the same time. It is mostly used with projects requiring a thin piece of wood or plywood.

Angels and Horse Ornaments

Here's how:

1. Instructions for making each ornament pattern are identical. Make photocopy of Angels and Horse Ornaments Patterns on page 41. Temporarily adhere one pattern onto ⅛" baltic birch plywood with spray adhesive. (Refer to Simple Fish, Steps 3–5 on page 24.) Tape second or third plywood piece securely to pattern piece with masking tape (see picture below). In pictured example, author is using a ¼" piece of plywood with two ⅛" pieces. Stack-sawing in this manner gives support to such thin plywood.

Continued on page 40

Above, finished project size: ⅛" x 5¹⁄₁₆" x 4". White acrylic spray paint finish.

Continued from page 38

2. Use awl to mark drill guides within areas to be cut out (see picture below).

3. Using ⅟₁₆" bit, drill blade-entry/threading holes (see picture below).

4. Install #5 reverse-tooth blade in scroll saw. Cut away interior areas first, then cut along outside edge. (Refer to Scotty Dog and Lucky Cat, Steps 5–6 on pages 26–27.)

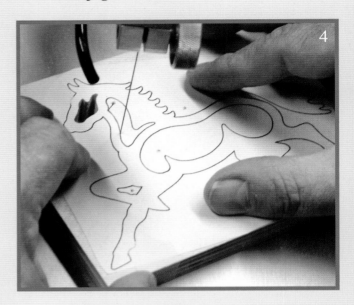

5. Remove pattern and masking tape. Separate wood pieces and touch up any imperfections with sandpaper and needle files. Finish sanding to desired smoothness.

6. Apply white acrylic spray paint finish. (Refer to Project Finishing on page 19.)

Above, horse ornament with Danish oil finish

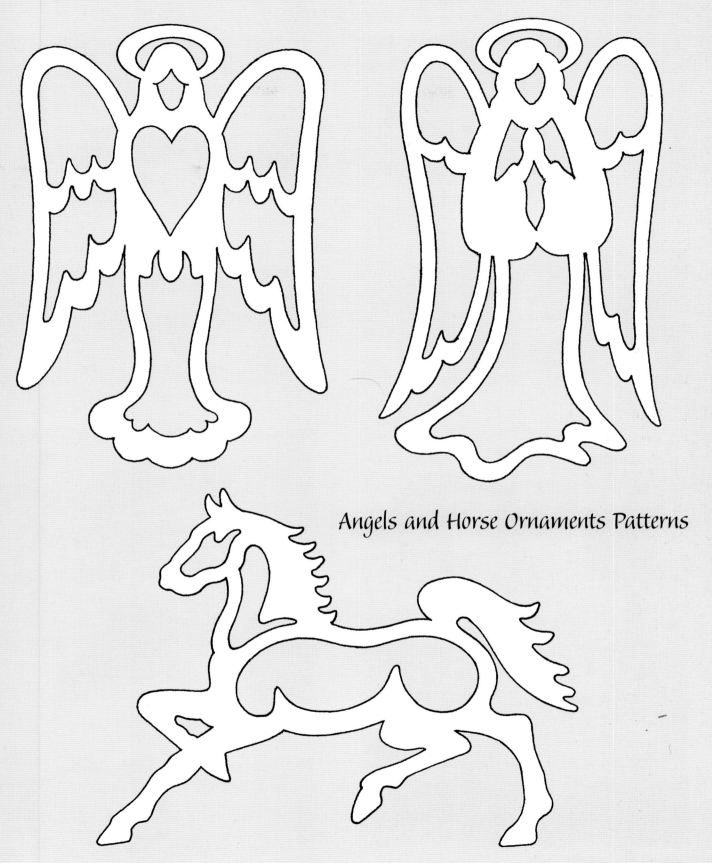

Angels and Horse Ornaments Patterns

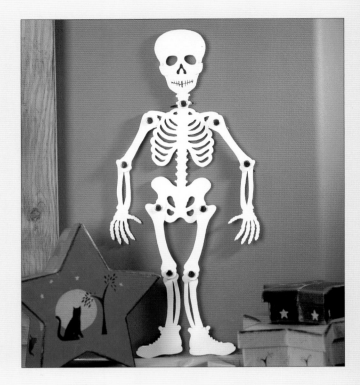

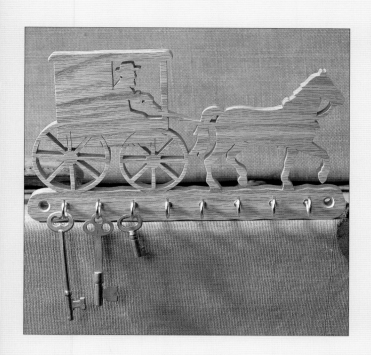

Section 3: Beyond the Basics

Expanding your skills

Simple, basic projects are fun and relatively easy to make. Some people enjoy doing simple projects as a break or respite from large and complex projects while others are perfectly happy remaining at this level with their scroll saw. There are many patterns available for this level of craftsman.

However, in this book, we want to show how easy it is to continue expanding your horizons and your scroll-saw skills. We want to show you how to produce all kinds of amazing projects with just a few more tools, a couple of handy tips, and some truly interesting patterns.

A handy scroll-saw tool kit

In addition to the Basic Tools and Supplies mentioned on page 13, a few additions to your toolbox should be made in anticipation of more demanding projects (see picture below).

Above, cards, needle-nosed pliers, a red pen, masking tape, and packaging tape are all necessary items in your toolbox.

Your toolbox should include:
• Needle-nosed pliers to straighten or remove bent or broken blades.
• Business card or playing card to tape over the opening on the saw table. Pierce a hole through it with an awl to make a zero clearance support around the blade, to support tiny, fragile parts.
• Red ink pen for altering patterns and producing "new" lines to saw along.
• Masking tape for holding stacks of material together, mending patterns, etc.
• Clear packaging tape for covering patterns to lubricate the blade and prevent it from making burn marks in the wood.
Plus, any other handy item that you may find yourself needing almost every time you are cutting something on your scroll saw.

Drills and bits

In the previous section, you used a hand drill and bits to make a few holes. Now you will want to add a drill press to your workshop and expand your selection of drill bits to include a wider variety of

sizes and styles (see picture at right). Handheld drills work fine with simple projects, but a drill press helps when working on very detailed work. A drill press is suited for the drilling of straight holes through all types of material. It is

Above, a drill press is an important addition to your workshop.

especially recommended when using Forstner bits, which remove large amounts of material and can easily grab and twist unsecured material. Forstner bits are often used to bore cavities for mounting clock and photo inserts.

In order to make cut out areas, you must drill blade-entry holes to thread the scroll-saw blade through the wood. A typical small set of drill bits usually includes sizes ranging from ⅟₁₆" to ½". Since you will often work with small cut-out areas, you will need smaller diameter bits. Although a ⅟₁₆" bit may have seemed very small to you up to now, you will find that you will need to acquire much smaller sizes, including a ⅟₃₂" bit, as well as mini-drill bits which are usually sold in wire-gauge sizes. Mini-drill sizes most commonly used among scroll-saw craftsmen are #60, #65, and #70 (see picture below).

Above, mini-drill bits like the ones shown spilling out of the red tube are used by scroll-saw artists.

NOTE: Always use a backer board (a scrap piece of wood) under your workpiece when drilling. It will help reduce tear-out on the bottom side when the drill bit exits the wood.

Cleaning up your work

As you strive to improve the appearance of each new project you are cutting out, by polishing your sawing techniques, be aware of the importance of taking time to clean up any of your "sawing imperfections" with sandpaper, needle files, craft knives and other tools that are available.

A set of needle files is ideally suited for getting inside tiny scroll-sawn "cut-out" openings.

Reciprocating tools, like a motorized file are designed to hold needle files, rasps, sanding paddles, and other accessories. They make the sanding job much easier and faster (see picture below).

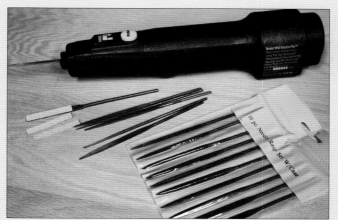

Above, a reciprocating tool and needle files are great tools for smoothing out scroll-sawn imperfections.

A belt/disc sander is also a terrific addition to your scroll-saw workshop. Use it to remove humps, bumps, and imperfections on straight edges; smooth out curves; adjust the base on a project to make it stand straight; dress up flat surfaces and edges, and much more.

Of course, there are many other tools available for sanding, shaping, and polishing your projects. You can do it all by hand to get you started. Then if this looks like a hobby that you are really going to enjoy, you should have no trouble finding the right tools.

1
Project

What you need to get started:

Tools:
- Basic tools and supplies page 13
- Photocopier
- Scroll saw with #5 reverse-tooth blade
- Power drill with $\frac{5}{32}$", $\frac{1}{8}$", and countersink bits
- Foam brush

Materials:
- $\frac{1}{4}$" x 5½" x 9" clear pine board
- (2) #4 x ⅝" flat-head wood screws

How do I make a decorative shelf with an attractive support bracket?

A simple shelf bracket is easy to make and attach to your shelf. It makes the shelf stronger and more attractive.

Fleur-de-lis Wall Shelf

Here's how:

1. Photocopy Fleur-de-lis Wall Shelf Patterns on page 49. Using scissors, trim patterns and position pattern for shelf onto wood to take advantage of a straight edge (see picture below). Temporarily adhere patterns onto wood with spray adhesive. (Refer to Simple Fish, Steps 4–5 on page 24.)

2. Install #5 reverse-tooth blade in scroll saw. Since there are no cut-out openings, cut on all outer lines to create back piece, shelf, and the bracket. (Refer to Scroll-sawing Techniques, Step 5 on pages 17–18.) Before removing patterns, use awl to mark locations for the hanging hole, and mounting holes. (Refer to Maple Leaf Shelf, Step 3 on page 35.)

Continued on page 48

Above, finished project size: ¼" x 5¼" x 6⅜". Natural Danish oil finish.

Continued from page 46

3. Use awl marks as guides to drill two ⅛" holes for mounting screws and one ⁵⁄₃₂"-diameter hanging hole. On back side, use a countersink bit to set screw heads flush with surface. (Refer to Maple Leaf Shelf, Step 4 on page 35.)

4. Use carpenter's square to check that back edge and top of bracket are perfectly square (see picture below). Adjust top edge as needed by drawing a new cutting line and recutting if necessary. Also, make certain top edge is straight and flat. *NOTE:* A belt/disc sander works great for making these kinds of adjustments.

5. Remove patterns from wood. Touch up any imperfections with sandpaper. Finish sanding all parts to desired smoothness. (Refer to Project Finishing on page 18.)

6. Mark and drill ¹⁄₁₆" pilot holes in the edge of shelf to line up with holes in the back piece. (Refer to Maple Leaf Shelf, Step 7 on page 35.)

7. Test-fit shelf by temporarily installing the mounting screws. Set bracket in position under shelf. Make adjustments as needed by reaming out pilot holes in the shelf (or redrilling them straighter). Remove screws, apply a small amount of wood glue to edge of shelf, and securely fasten back together again with mounting screws. Apply a small amount of wood glue to back and top of the bracket, then carefully place in position. Apply a little pressure and hold in place for a few seconds.

8. After glue dries, apply finish. Natural Danish oil finish is applied with a rag or foam brush, then allowed to dry for a few minutes. Wipe excess oil off with a clean rag. (Refer to Project Finishing on page 19.)
   NOTE: You may enlarge the patterns as needed to make larger shelves. A proportion scale (see picture below) is available from many craft and hobby stores. It makes calculation of enlargement and reduction of patterns easy.

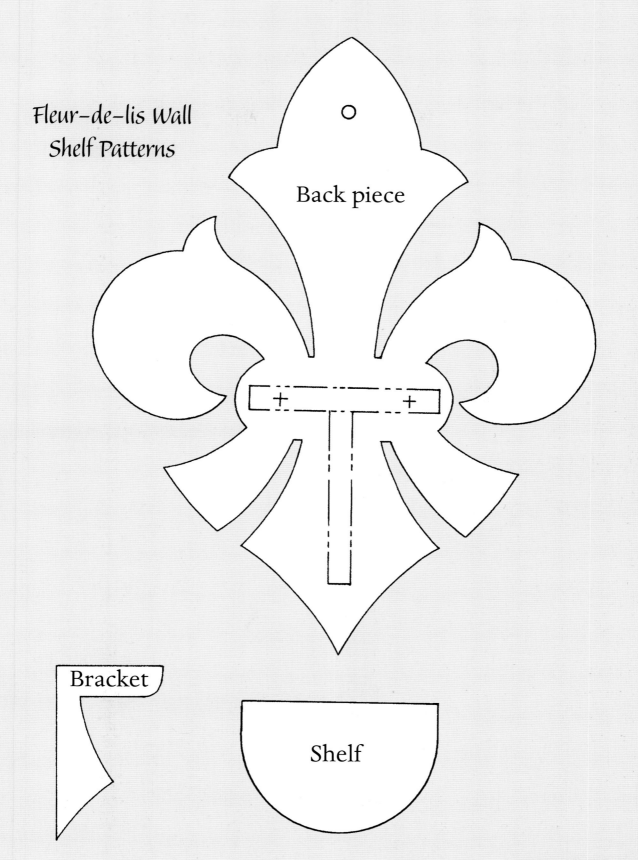

Fleur-de-lis Wall
Shelf Patterns

Back piece

Bracket

Shelf

2
Project

What you need to get started:

Tools:
- Basic tools and supplies page 13
- Photocopier
- Scroll saw with #5 reverse-tooth blade
- Drill with ⁵⁄₃₂" and countersink bits, and optional 1⅜" Forstner bit
- 1¹⁷⁄₁₆" diameter clock insert
- Foam Brush

Materials:
- ¾" x 5½" x 6¼" pine
- ¾" x 2½" x 7" pine
- (2) #6 x ¾" flat-head wood screws

How do I turn my scroll–saw project into a clock?

To put a clock in a scroll-saw project, you can simply cut a hole—or use a Forstner bit to make a cavity for the clock insert to fit in.

Mighty Moose

Here's how:

1. Photocopy Mighty Moose Patterns on page 54. Temporarily adhere patterns onto wood with spray adhesive. (Refer to Simple Fish, Steps 3–5 on page 24.) Place bottom of pattern for moose along straight finished edge (see picture below).

2. Use awl to mark locations for blade-entry holes in areas to be cut out (between legs and eye). Mark center points for holes in base for mounting screws.

Continued on page 52

Above, finished project size: ¾" x 6⅜" x 5⅞". Natural Danish oil finish.

Continued from page 46

3. Moose can be made with or without clock insert. Create mounting hole by carefully cutting out a circle with #5 reverse-tooth blade (see picture 3a below). Do not cut outside of the pattern line, or insert may fit too loosely. Stay slightly inside cutting line. Test-fit insert and adjust mounting hole as needed. If insert fits too tightly, opening can be enlarged by sanding.

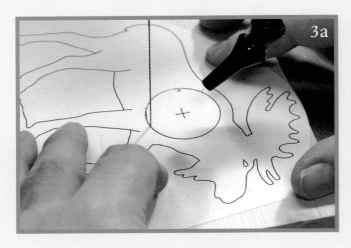

Another option (for those who have gained experience using various woodworking tools, is to use a 1⅜" Forstner bit to bore a cavity (see picture 3b below).

Forstner bits should be used in a drill press. Large-diameter bits can easily grab and turn the workpiece from your hands, so make certain wood is securely clamped to drill-press table. Use awl to mark center point for mounting hole, which will serve as guide for bit. Bore mounting cavity before any scroll-saw cutting (see picture 3c below).

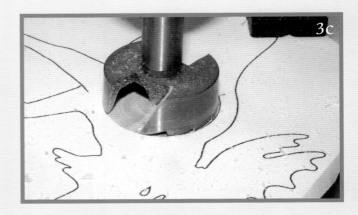

4. To cut out pieces, use scroll saw with #5 reverse-tooth blade. Cut out openings within the piece at eye and between legs. (Refer to Scotty Dog and Lucky Cat, Steps 4–6 on pages 26–27.) Cut around outer profile of moose, then cut around the base.

5. Drill two ⁵⁄₃₂" holes through base for mounting screws. Countersink so screw heads are flush with bottom surface of base (see picture below).

6. Lay bottom edge of moose along the holes in base, centered left to right. Use pencil to mark centers of pilot holes to be drilled into bottom edge of moose (see picture below).

7. Use a ruler to measure center of wood and mark center points. Use awl to make indentation on each center point. Drill ⅟₁₆" holes to accept tips of mounting screws.

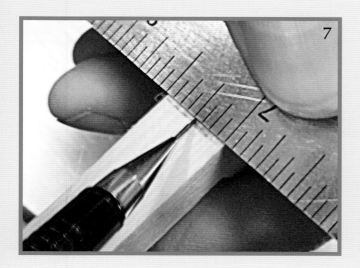

8. Remove patterns from wood. Touch up any imperfections with sandpaper. Finish sanding all parts to desired smoothness. (Refer to Project Finishing on page 18.)

9. Test-fit moose to base and temporarily install mounting screws. Make adjustments as needed. When satisfied with fit, remove screws, apply a small amount of wood glue to bottom of moose and reassemble with mounting screws. Wipe away excess glue.

10. When glue has dried, apply finish. Natural Danish oil finish is applied with a rag or foam brush, then allowed to dry for a few minutes. Wipe excess oil off with a clean rag.
   NOTE: Other possible finishes may include stain, paint, or even varnish. (Refer to Project Finishing on page 19.)

Above, Mighty Moose without the clock insert and sporting a distressed paint finish.

Mighty Moose Patterns

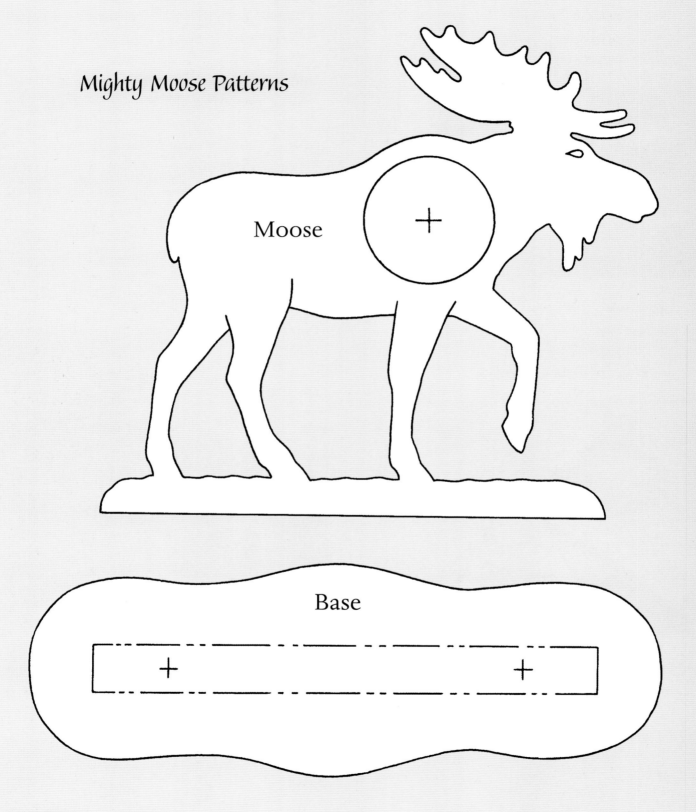

Moose

Base

How can I make scroll–sawn shapes more interesting?

There are many scroll-saw designs that utilize interior cutouts to add interest to the piece.

Mini Duck

Here's how:

1. Photocopy Mini Duck Patterns on page 58. Take advantage of straight edges on wood to place patterns for duck and cattails. Temporarily adhere patterns onto wood with spray adhesive. (Refer to Simple Fish, Steps 3–5 on page 24.)

2. Use awl to mark drill guides within areas to be cut out, and for mounting screws in base. If boring clock cavity with Forstner bit, mark center spot for bit.

3. If you choose to bore a mounting cavity, do so prior to scroll sawing. Clamp wood onto drill press table and use 1⅜" Forstner bit to bore cavity. Otherwise, install #5 reverse-tooth blade in scroll saw and carefully cut hole. Stay slightly inside of line (see picture below).

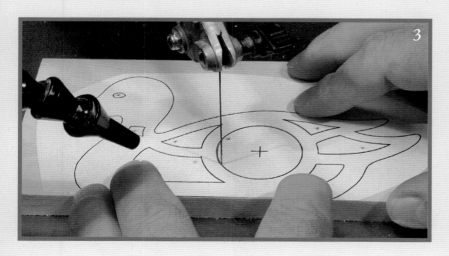

What you need to get started:

Tools:
- Basic tools and supplies page 13
- Photocopier
- Scroll saw with #5 reverse-tooth blades
- Drill press with 1⅜" Forstner bit, countersink, 1/16", and 5/32" bits
- 1 17/16" diameter clock insert
- Needle files

Materials:
- Duck ½" x 3½" x 6¾" pine
- Cattails ½" x 2½" x 6" pine
- Base ½" x 3" x 7¼" pine
- (3) #6 x ¾" flat-head wood screws

Above, finished project size: ½" x 7" x 3¾". Acrylic paint finish.

4. Make interior cuts first, then cut around contour lines.

5. Drill three ⁵⁄₃₂" holes through base for mounting screws. Countersink for screw heads on bottom side of base.

6. Remove patterns. Clean up any cutting imperfections with sandpaper, needle files, etc. Finish sanding all parts to desired smoothness. (Refer to Project Finishing on page 18.)

7. Make pilot holes for mounting screws in bottom edges of duck and cattails. Lay duck and cattails pieces flat along existing holes in base, and make pencil marks to line up with centers of base holes (see picture below).

8. Measure and mark to center of wood to locate points for pilot holes. Use awl to make indentation to serve as drilling guide (see picture below). Bore the holes approximately ¼" deep with a ¹⁄₁₆" bit.

9. Test-fit duck and cattails onto base. Install mounting screws. Make adjustments as needed. When satisfied with fit, apply small amount of wood glue to joints and secure with mounting screws. Wipe away excess glue.

10. Apply acrylic paint with paintbrush to color duck and cattails as shown in photograph on page 56. (Refer to Project Finishing on page 19.)

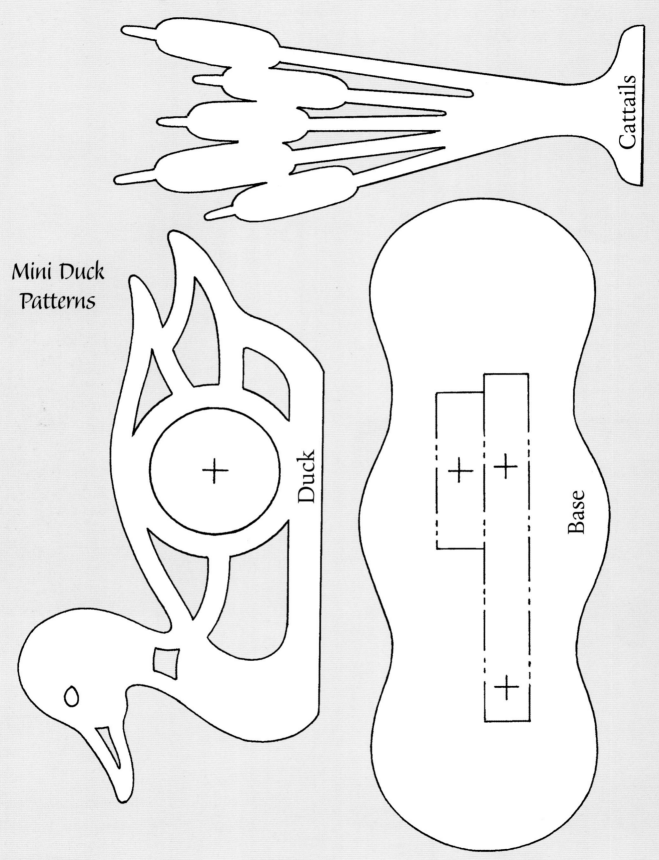

Mini Duck
Patterns

Cattails

Duck

Base

How can I give my scroll–saw designs more detail?

It is possible to make definition lines, or single saw cut lines, to give your piece more detail.

Amish Buggy Utility Hanger

Here's how:

1. Photocopy Amish Buggy Utility Hanger Pattern on page 62. Temporarily adhere patterns onto wood with spray adhesive. (Refer to Simple Fish, Steps 3–5 on page 24.)

2. Use awl to mark drill guides within areas to be cut out (see picture below).

What you need to get started:

Tools:
- Basic tools and supplies page 13
- Photocopier
- Scroll saw with #5 reverse-tooth blades
- Drill with $\frac{1}{16}$", $\frac{3}{32}$", and $\frac{7}{32}$" bits
- Needle files
- Foam brush

Materials:
- $\frac{1}{2}$" x $5\frac{1}{4}$" x $9\frac{1}{4}$" oak
- Natural Danish oil
- (8) Brass cup hooks
- (2) #10 x $1\frac{1}{4}$" mounting screws with wall anchors

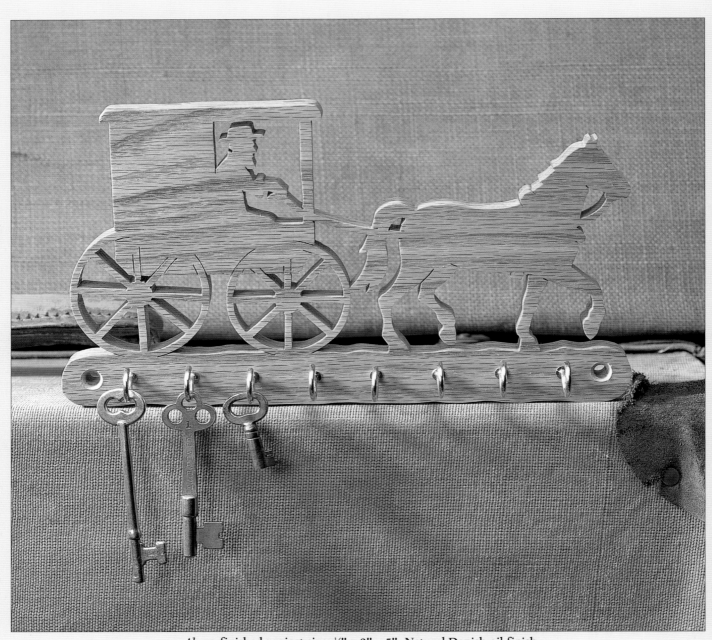

Above, finished project size: ½" x 9" x 5". Natural Danish oil finish.

3. Using ⅟₁₆" bit, drill blade-entry holes through all cutout areas (see picture below). Use ⁷⁄₃₂" bit to bore the two outermost holes for mounting screws. Use ³⁄₃₂" bit to drill eight pilot holes for cup hooks.

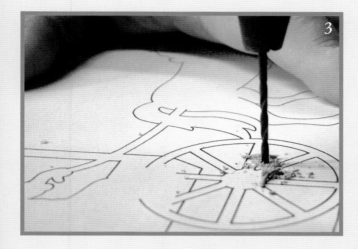

4. Install #5 reverse-tooth blade in scroll saw. Make all interior cuts first, then finish cutting around the outside. (Refer to Scotty Dog and Lucky Cat, Steps 5–6 on pages 26–27.)

5. Remove pattern. Touch up any imperfections with sandpaper, needle files, etc. Finish sanding to desired smoothness (see picture below). (Refer to Project Finishing on page 18.)

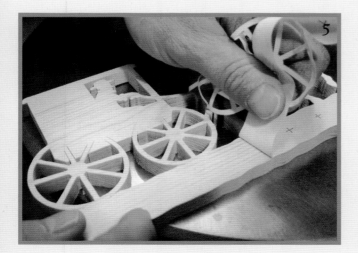

6. Using clean rag or foam brush, apply coat of natural Danish oil finish. Allow to dry for a few minutes, then wipe off excess oil. (Refer to Project Finishing on page 19.)

7. Install cup hooks by hand by turning them into predrilled pilot holes (see picture below). *NOTE:* If hook is too difficult to turn by hand, use pliers with a thick rag inside pliers jaws to prevent scratching brass hooks.

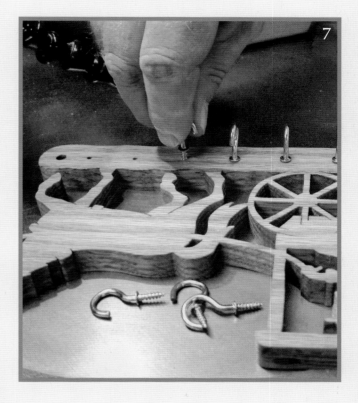

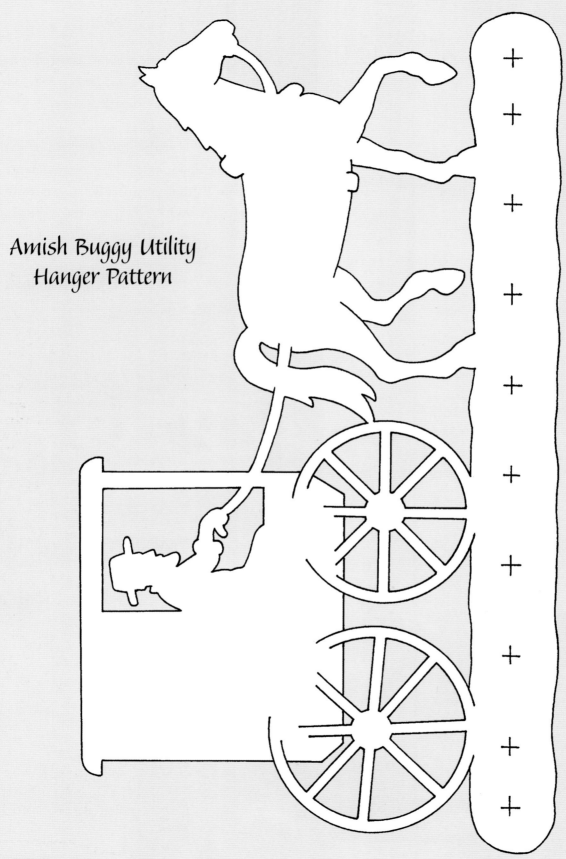

Amish Buggy Utility
Hanger Pattern

How can I make a scroll-saw picture?

Scroll-saw pictures are easy to make provided you start with a good pattern. This particular pattern is self-framing, so the outside must be perfectly square from the start.

Big Buck

Here's how:

1. Make a photocopy of Big Buck Pattern on page 66. Use ruler to measure photocopy to get exact outside dimensions (ours is 6⅝" x 9", yours may be slightly different due to copier distortion). Precut two pieces of wood to exact size of pattern. The process of stacksawing will be used to produce two projects simultaneously. Use carpenter's square to make certain that all four corners are cut perfectly square.

    NOTE: A table saw or radial arm saw are the best tools for making straight, square cuts. If you do not have these tools the project may be cut with a scroll saw. For this job, use #7 reverse-tooth blade in scroll saw because larger blades work best for cutting straight lines.

2. Trim pattern closely with scissors. Cut several notches in outside border to make it easier to position pattern on wood. Temporarily adhere the pattern onto one piece of wood with spray adhesive. (Refer to Simple Fish, Steps 4–5 on page 24.)

What you need to get started:

Tools:
- Basic tools and supplies page 13
- Photocopier
- Scroll saw with #2 and #5 reverse-tooth blades
- Drill with ¹⁄₁₆" bit and #65 mini-drill bit
- Needle files
- Craft knife
- Foam brush

Materials:
- (2) ¼" x 6⅝" x 9" Baltic birch plywood, pine, oak
- Natural Danish oil
- Sawtooth hanger and mounting nails

Above, finished project size: ¼" x 6⅜" x 9". Natural Danish oil finish.

3. Place second piece of wood under pattern piece. Line up all edges, and wrap short lengths of masking tape around them to hold both pieces of wood tightly together (see picture below). Two or three pieces of tape around each side is sufficient to hold wood together.

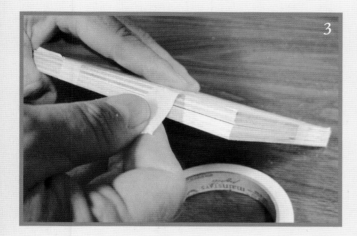

4. On this project, some openings for saw-blade insertion are very small. To make blade-entry holes in these areas, use tiny drill bits. For example, drill blade entry holes for the eyes, ears, nose, neck, rear leg, and antler with #65 mini-drill bit (see picture below). Make certain these small holes extend completely through wood. The balance of saw-blade insertion holes may be drilled with ⅟₁₆" bit.

5. Cut out openings within the piece. (Refer to Scotty Dog and Lucky Cat, Steps 3–6 on pages 26–27.) Use #2 reverse-tooth blade for small openings. For larger openings, use #5 reverse-tooth blade. After completing all cutouts, cut off four rounded corners on outer edge.

6. After cutting is complete, remove pattern and masking tape (see picture below). Separate pieces. Touch up any imperfections with sand-paper, needle files, etc. Finish sanding all surfaces to desired smooth-ness. (Refer to Project Finishing on page 18.)

7. Using clean rag or foam brush, apply coat of natural Danish oil finish. Allow to dry for a few minutes, then wipe off excess oil. (Refer to Project Finishing on page 19.)

8. When dry, measure to find top center on back of project. Install sawtooth hanger. Predrill pilot holes for mounting nails, and fasten hanger securely in place (see picture below).

Big Buck Pattern

How can I accurately make two objects with a mirror image?

Stack-sawing is a technique that can also be used to make accurate mirror images.

Dynamic Dragon Duo

Here's how:

1. Place best sides of wood together "face-to-face" toward inside (see picture below).

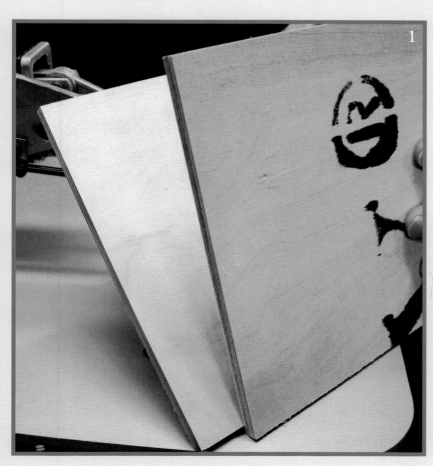

6
Project

What you need to get started:

Tools:
- Basic tools and supplies page 13
- Photocopier
- Scroll saw with #5 reverse-tooth blade
- Drill with ⅟₁₆" bit
- Needle files

Materials:
- (2) ¼" x 6½" x 9" Baltic birch plywood
- Packaging tape
- Natural Danish oil
- Frame with contrasting colored backing

Above, finished project size in frame: 1" x 16¼" x 13⅛". Natural Danish oil finish.

2. Photocopy Dynamic Dragon Duo Pattern on page 70. Temporarily adhere patterns onto wood with spray adhesive. (Refer to Simple Fish, Steps 3–5 on page 24.) Tape strips of masking tape around edges of both pieces of wood to hold together (see picture below). Cover pattern with layer of clear packaging tape. This tape will lubricate blade while cutting and prevent blade from burning wood.

3. Use awl to mark drill guides within areas to be cut out. Using 1/16" bit, drill blade-entry holes through all cutout areas.

4. Install #5 reverse-tooth blade in scroll saw. Start by making all cut-out openings. (Refer to Scotty Dog and Lucky Cat, Steps 3–6 on pages 26–27.) *NOTE:* This project features a few "definition lines." These lines add detail to the project, and are basically just single saw cuts. These lines help to accent the belly, legs, wings, etc.

5. Remove pattern and tape. Separate dragons exposing good side of wood from inside the stack. This creates a pair of facing dragons (see picture below).

6. Touch up any cutting imperfections with sandpaper, needle files, etc. (Refer to Project Finishing on page 18.)

7. Using brush or clean rag, apply coat of natural Danish oil finish. Allow to dry for a few minutes, then wipe off excess oil. (Refer to Project Finishing on page 19.)

8. Hang the dragons on the wall, as is, or mount within a frame on a backing of colored or contrasting material.

Dynamic Dragon Duo Pattern

(Cut 2)

Dragon

How can I tell if a scroll–saw pattern is going to be simple or challenging?

Small intricate cuts, such as those found on a face, and long sweeping curves always take an extra measure of skill and patience.

Hope Angels

Here's how:

1. Photocopy Hope Angels Pattern on page 74. Temporarily adhere patterns onto wood with spray adhesive. (Refer to Simple Fish, Steps 3–5 on page 24.)

2. Prepare "stack" by applying masking tape around edges of wood (see picture below). Cover pattern with clear packaging tape to lubricate blade and prevent burning wood along edges.

7
Project

What you need to get started:

Tools:

• Basic tools and supplies page 13

• Photocopier

• Scroll saw with #2 and #5 reverse-tooth blades

• Drill press with #61 mini-drill and ¹⁄₁₆" bits

• Needle files

Materials:

• (2) ¼" x 7¼" x 8¼" Baltic birch plywood

• Packaging tape

• White matte acrylic spray paint

Above, finished project size: ¼" x 7⅞" x 7". Natural Danish oil finish.

3. Use awl to mark drill guides within areas to be cut out (see picture below).

4. Drill blade-entry holes for angel eyes with #61 mini-drill bit. Use ⅟₁₆" bit for remainder of holes (see picture below).

5. Install #2 reverse-tooth blade in scroll saw, and use it to cut out openings for the eyes.
   NOTE: You may want to use this same blade to cut a few of the other smaller openings. (Refer to Scotty Dog and Lucky Cat, Steps 3–6 on pages 26–27.)

6. Install #5 reverse-tooth blade to make remaining cutouts and for cutting around the outside of the project.

7. Remove the pattern. Touch up any imperfections with sandpaper, needle files, etc. Finish sanding to desired smoothness. (Refer to Project Finishing on page 18.)

8. Use white matte acrylic spray paint to lightly color Hope Angels. Allow wood grain to show through to give piece an antique effect. (Refer to Project Finishing on page 19.)
   NOTE: This piece would also look terrific painted bright white with a subtle mist of spray glitter applied onto top.

Above, Hope Angels also look wonderful with a natural Danish oil finish.

Handmade Christmas ornaments are very popular. How can I make them quickly?

8

Project

Stack-sawing can help make the cutting go quickly. Painting or staining the figures in various ways will give individuality and variety to your ornaments.

Ornaments and More Ornaments

Here's how:

1. Photocopy Ornaments and More Ornaments Patterns on page 77. Temporarily adhere patterns onto wood with spray adhesive. (Refer to Simple Fish, Steps 3–5 on page 24.)

2. Prepare "stack" by tightly wrapping short lengths of masking tape around edges of the wood to hold all four pieces securely together (see picture below). Cover top of pattern with clear packaging tape to lubricate the blade while cutting, and prevent burning.

What you need to get started:

Tools:
- Basic tools and supplies page 13
- Photocopier
- Scroll saw with #2 and #5 reverse-tooth blades
- Drill press with #61 mini-drill, ⁵⁄₃₂", and ¹⁄₁₆" bits
- Needle files

Materials:
- (4) ⅛" x 6¾" x 9¼" Baltic birch plywood
- Packaging tape
- Acrylic paints
- Stains
- Natural Danish oil
- White acrylic spray paint
- Hanging wires, beads, etc.

Above, finished project size: ⅛" x 3¼" x 2½". Acrylic paint finish.

3. Use awl to mark drill guides within areas to be cut out.

4. Select drill bits to fit within the areas to be cut out, and bore holes as needed. Also, drill holes for hangers.

5. Install #2 reverse-tooth blade in scroll saw to cut out inside openings. Use #5 reverse-tooth blade to cut outside contour lines.

6. Remove patterns. Touch up any imperfections with sandpaper or needle files. Finish sanding to desired smoothness. (Refer to Project Finishing on page 18.)

7. Use paintbrush and acrylic paints to color ornaments. Vary colors or use stains or Danish oil to give ornaments variety and character. Ornaments can also be spray painted white. (Refer to Project Finishing on page 19.)

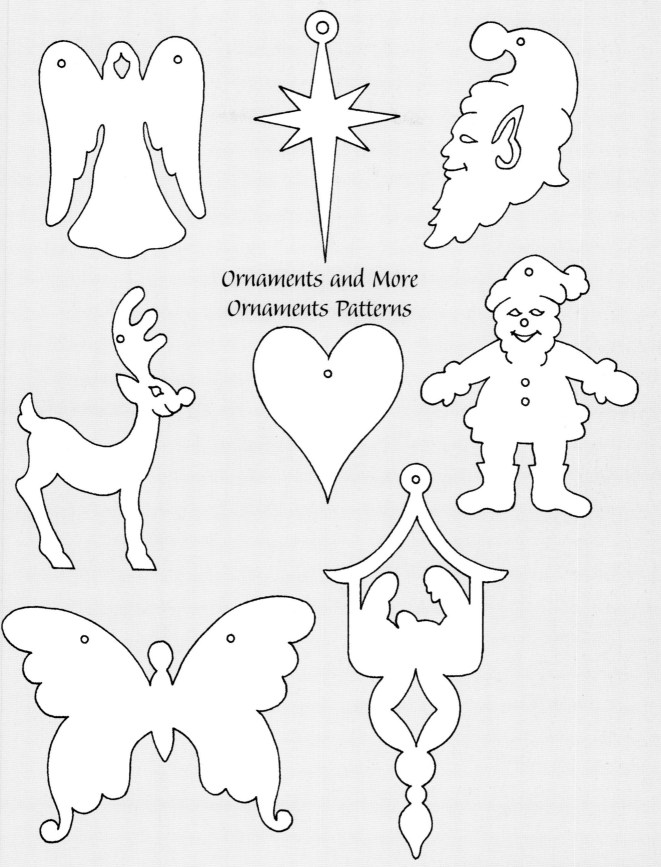

Ornaments and More
Ornaments Patterns

9
Project

What you need to get started:

Tools:
- Basic tools and supplies page 13
- Photocopier
- Scroll saw with #2 and #5 reverse-tooth blade
- Power drill with $\frac{1}{32}$", $\frac{1}{16}$", and $\frac{1}{8}$" bits

Materials:
- Head (3) $\frac{1}{8}$" x $2\frac{3}{4}$" x $4\frac{3}{4}$" Baltic birch plywood
- Body (3) $\frac{1}{8}$" x 4" x $6\frac{3}{4}$" Baltic birch plywood
- Arms and legs (3) $\frac{1}{8}$" x 7" x $9\frac{1}{4}$" Baltic birch plywood
- Needle files
- (9) Brass fasteners 1" with $\frac{3}{8}$" brass top
- Satin white spray enamel

How do I make a project with moveable parts?

Stack-sawing some decorative skeletons not only gives you a project with moveable parts, but it gives you several copies all at once.

Mr. Bones

Here's how:

1. Use masking tape to securely fasten each stack of three pieces of plywood together.

2. Photocopy Mr. Bones Patterns on pages 80–81. Temporarily adhere patterns onto appropriate plywood stacks with spray adhesive (Refer to Simple Fish, Steps 3–5 on page 24).

3. Use awl to make an indentation wherever cut-out openings are to be made. Also, mark center points where brass fasteners will be installed to fasten body parts together.

4. Most blade-entry holes may be drilled with $\frac{1}{16}$" bit. Use $\frac{1}{32}$" bit to bore hole for the mouth and teeth area.
    NOTE: The teeth in the pattern on page 80 are somewhat difficult to saw. If you have any problems, use the Optional head pattern on page 81, which has a much simpler mouth. Openings for fasteners should be drilled with $\frac{1}{8}$" bit.

5. Install #2 reverse-tooth blade in scroll saw to make cutouts for teeth. (Refer to Scotty Dog and Lucky Cat, Steps 3–6 on pages 26–27.) Install #5 reverse-tooth blade to make remainder of cutouts and to complete outside contour lines.

Continued on page 80

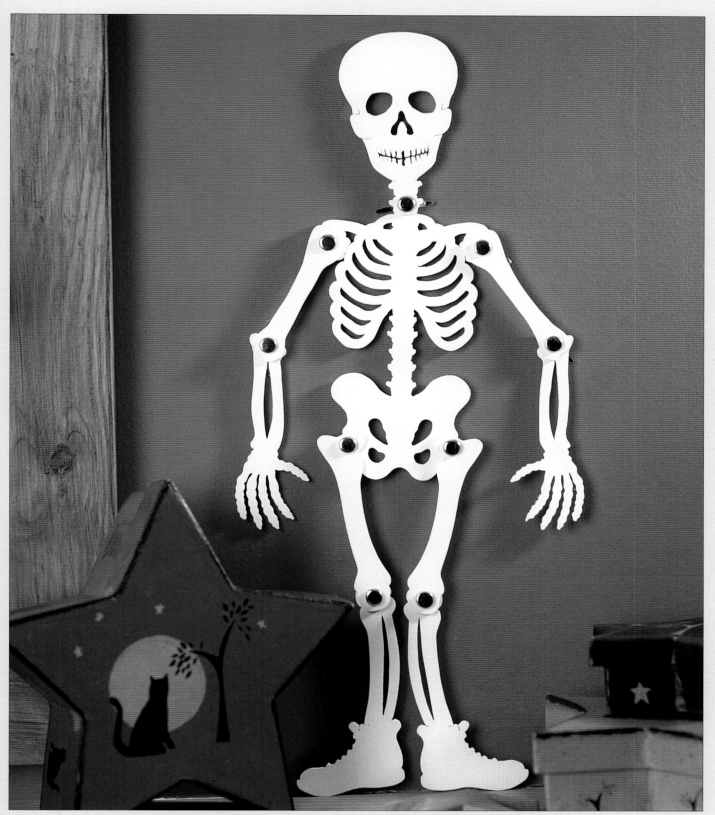

Above, finished project size: ⅛" x 4⅛" x 17⅛". Satin white spray enamel finish.

Continued from page 78

6. After cutting, remove patterns. Touch up any imperfections with sandpaper, needle files, etc. Finish sanding all surfaces to desired smoothness. (Refer to Project Finishing on page 18.)

7. Paint Mr. Bones with satin white spray enamel. (Refer to Project Finishing on page 19.)

8. Assemble skeleton pieces together with brass fasteners. Carefully insert ends through holes and bend ends in opposite directions to hold them in place (see picture right).

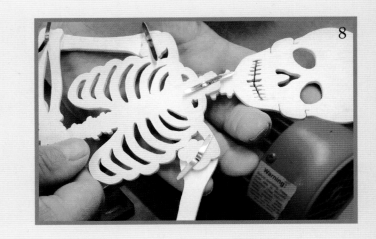

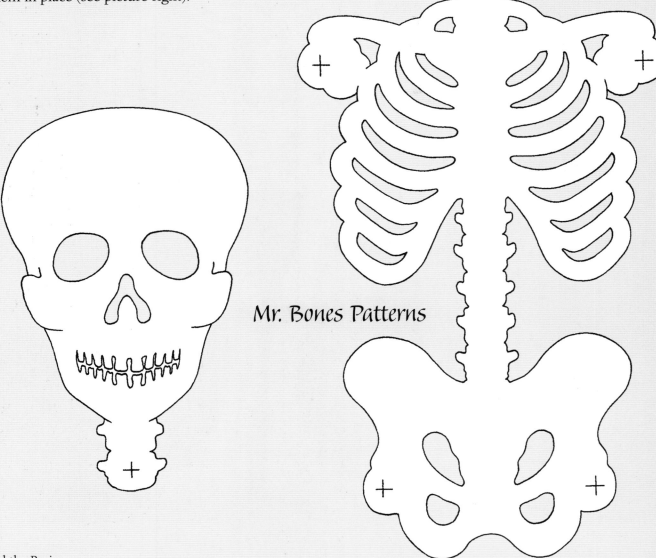

Mr. Bones Patterns

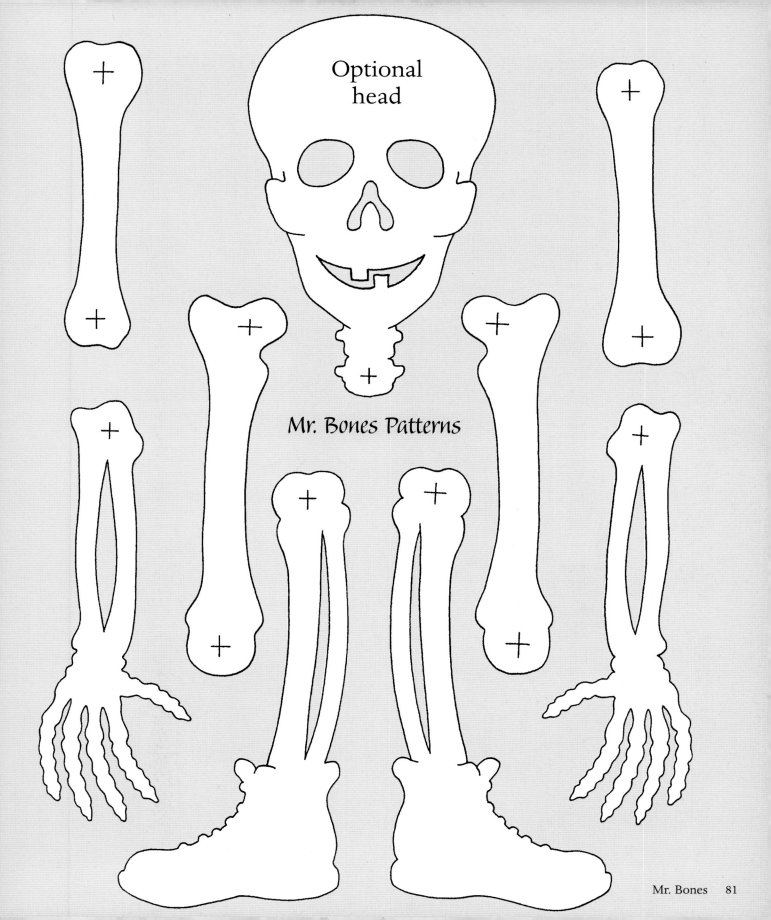

Optional head

Mr. Bones Patterns

Section 4: New Dimensions in Scroll Sawing

10 Project

What you need to get started:

Tools:
- Basic tools and supplies page 13
- Photocopier
- Scroll saw with #5 reverse-tooth blade
- Drill press with ⅟₁₆", ⅛", countersink and 1¹³⁄₁₆" Forstner bits
- Needle files
- Clamps
- Foam brush

Materials:
- ¼" x 7¼" x 9" poplar or oak
- ¾" x 2¼" x 8¾" poplar or oak
- (2) #4 x ⅝" flat-head wood screws
- Natural Danish oil
- 2" photo frame insert
- Photograph

How do I make a Victorian-style project?

Victorian-style scroll-sawn pieces usually have highly detailed floral patterns. This combination wall shelf and photo frame is perfect for a decoration of that period.

Miniature Victorian Wall Shelf and Photo Frame

Here's how:

1. Photocopy Miniature Victorian Wall Shelf and Photo Frame Patterns on pages 87–88. Temporarily adhere patterns onto wood with spray adhesive. (Refer to Simple Fish, Steps 3–5 on page 24.) Take advantage of straight edges for positioning patterns for the shelf and brackets (see picture below). Brackets can be stack-sawn if desired.

Continued on page 86

Above, finished project size: 2¼" x 8¾" x 7". Natural Danish oil finish.

Continued from page 84

2. Use awl to mark drill guides within areas to be cut out, and for mounting screws for shelf. For boring photo insert cavity with Forstner bit, mark center spot for bit.

3. Use ⅟₁₆" bit to bore entry blade-entry holes. Use 1¹³⁄₁₆" Forstner bit to make hole for photo frame, or carefully saw out opening on scroll saw. Use ⅛" bit to make holes for the mounting screws. (Refer to Mighty Moose, Step 3 on page 52.)

4. Install #5 reverse-tooth blade in scroll saw, and cut out all parts for project.

5. After cutting, remove patterns and clean up any imperfections with sandpaper, needle files, etc. (Refer to Project Finishing on page 18.)

6. Place shelf flat on top of back piece with edge lined up along the holes for mounting screws. Use pencil to mark centers of holes on the edge of shelf (see picture below). Use ruler to measure to the center of wood, and mark center point for drilling pilot holes for screws. Bore holes with a ⅟₁₆" drill bit.

7. Use carpenter's square to check angle of brackets. (Refer to Fleur-de-lis Wall Shelf, Step 4 on page 48.) Make adjustments as needed to ensure that brackets will hold the shelf level and square (see picture below).

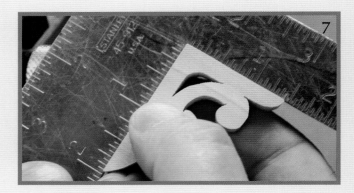

8. Test-fit shelf to back piece. Install mounting screws, making adjustments as needed. Set brackets, in place. If everything is satisfactory, take shelf apart and apply small amount of wood glue between shelf and back piece and screw back together. Brackets may be attached with glue only. Use clamps as needed to hold parts together until dry (see picture below).

9. Using clean rag or foam brush, apply coat of natural Danish oil finish. Allow to dry for a few minutes, then wipe off excess oil. (Refer to Project Finishing on page 19.)

Miniature Victorian Wall Shelf
and Photo Frame Patterns

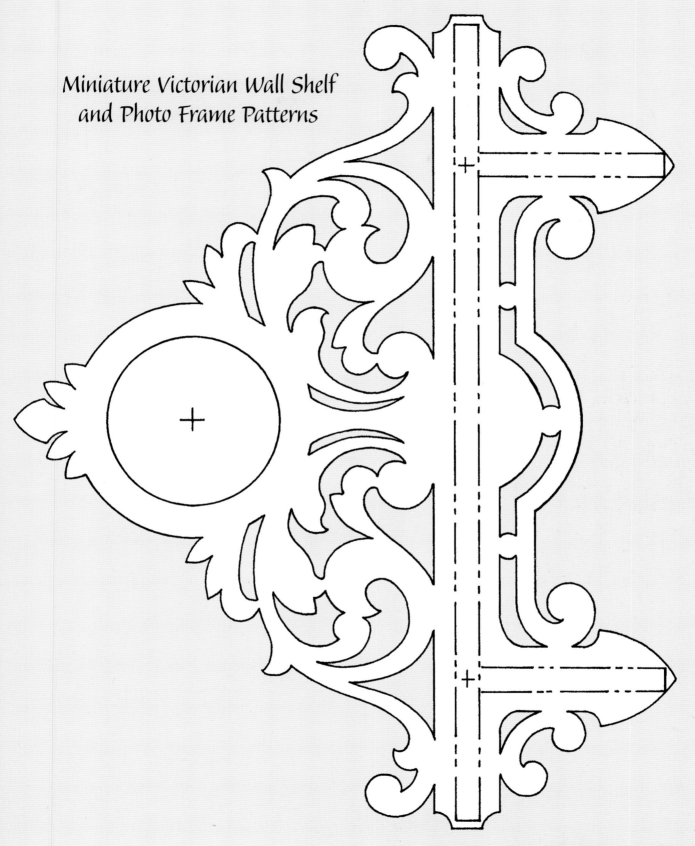

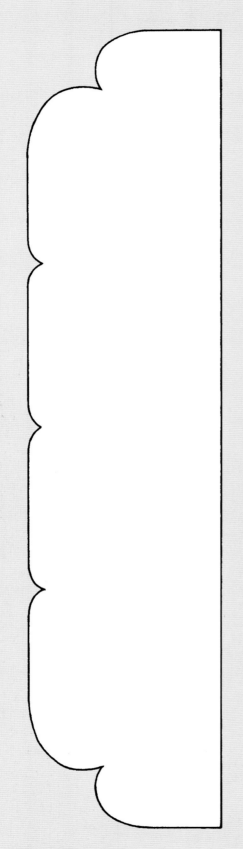

Miniature Victorian Wall Shelf and Photo Frame Patterns

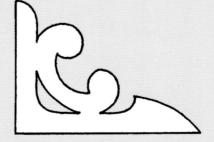

How can I use different types of wood to give my project contrasting natural colors?

Most woods work well together if the natural expansion and contraction of the wood is not an issue. When given a natural oil finish, the contrasting colors of various species of wood are very attractive. In this project a light-colored pine is put in contrast with a dark walnut.

Skull and Arrowhead

Here's how:

1. Photocopy Skull and Arrowhead Patterns on pages 91–93. Temporarily adhere patterns onto wood with spray adhesive. (Refer to Simple Fish, Steps 3–5 on page 24.) Feathers may be stack-sawn. (Refer to Angels and Horse Ornaments, Step 1 on page 38.)

2. Use awl to mark blade-entry holes and centers for holes on arrowhead for hanging.

3. Use ¹⁄₁₆" bit to make blade-entry holes. Use ⁵⁄₃₂" bit to make holes for hanging feathers.

4. Install #5 reverse-tooth blade in scroll saw and make all cutouts on skull. Also use #5 reverse-tooth blade to make cutouts in feathers, and to cut feather outlines. Install #7 reverse-tooth blade to cut outline of skull, and to cut out arrowhead.

What you need to get started:

Tools:
- Basic tools and supplies page 13
- Photocopier
- Scroll saw with #5 and #7 reverse-tooth blades
- Drill with ¹⁄₁₆" and ⁵⁄₃₂" bits
- Needle files
- Clamp
- Foam brush

Materials:
- Skull ¾" x 7¼" x 7¾" pine
- Arrowhead ¾" x 6¼" x 8¾" walnut
- Small feathers (4) ⅛" x 1¼" x 5½" Baltic birch plywood
- Large feathers (3) ⅛" x 1¾" x 7¾" Baltic birch plywood
- Natural Danish oil
- Leather lace

Above, finished project size: 1½" x 7" x 16½". Natural Danish oil finish.

5. After cutting, remove patterns and touch up any imperfections with sandpaper, needle files, etc. Finish sanding all parts to desired smoothness. (Refer to Project Finishing on page 18.)

6. Adhere skull to the arrowhead with wood glue. Clamp together with wood clamps, or set heavy object on top of skull and arrowhead, until dry.

7. Using clean rag or foam brush, apply coat of natural Danish oil finish to all pieces. Allow to dry for a few minutes, then wipe off excess oil. (Refer to Project Finishing on page 19.)

8. Hang large feathers from bottom of arrowhead by looping and tying with lengths of leather lace (see picture below).

9. Referring to finished project on page 90 for placement, loop lengths of leather to hang smaller feathers from horns (see picture below).

Skull and Arrowhead Patterns

(Cut 4)

(Cut 3)

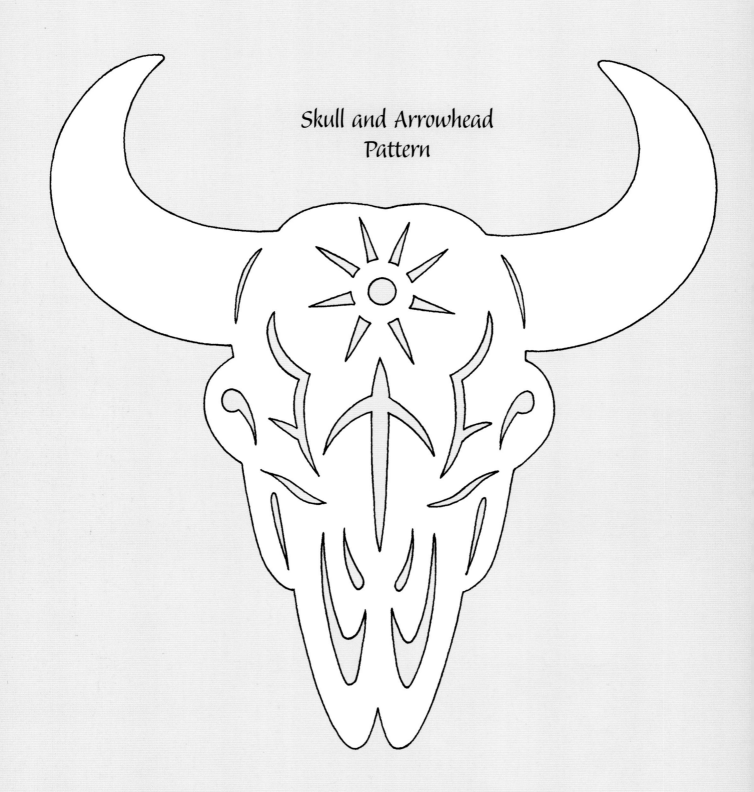

Skull and Arrowhead
Pattern

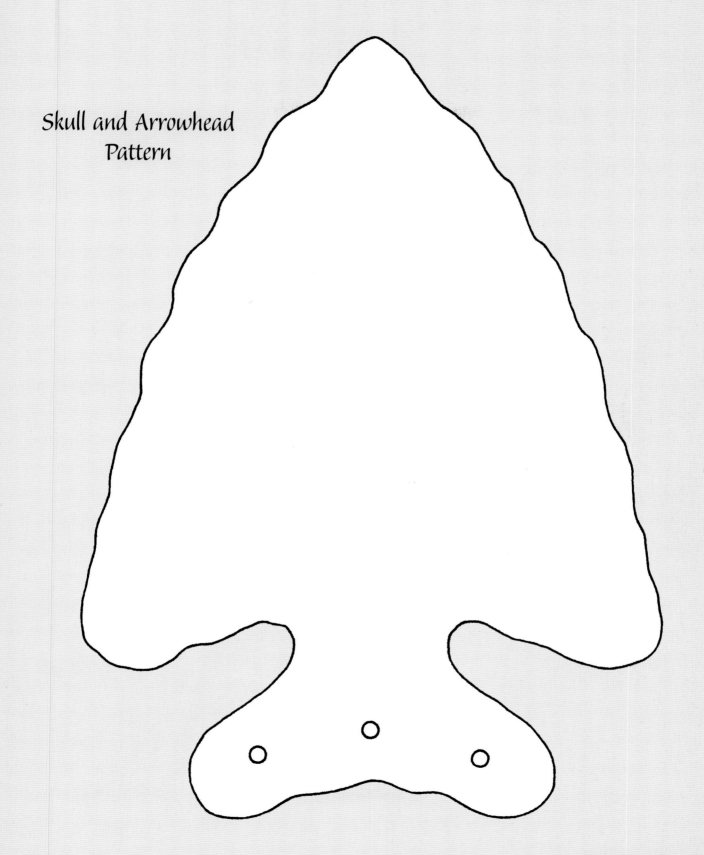

Skull and Arrowhead
Pattern

12
Project

What you need to get started:

Tools:
- Basic tools and supplies page 13
- Photocopier
- Scroll saw with #5 and #7 skip-tooth blades
- Drill with ⅟₁₆", ⁵⁄₆₄", and ⅛" bits
- Craft knife

Materials:
- Plexiglas, white translucent and red transparent
- Brass .015" thickness
- Scrap wood
- Packaging tape
- String
- Natural Danish oil, stain, or acrylic paint
- Notepads or stationery
- Cardboard

Can the scroll saw cut any— thing other than wood?

By using a few simple cutting techniques, the scroll saw can cut materials such as acrylic plastic (Plexiglas), thin brass, and paper.

Plexiglas Doves, Brass Crosses, and Paper Cutting

Here's how:

1. Photocopy Cross Pattern on page 97. Crosses are cut from thin brass and scraps of thin wood. Prepare a stack of three or four pieces of ⅛"-thick wood with a sheet of thin brass (.015") sandwiched in between. Adhere Cross Pattern to top of stack. (Refer to Simple Fish, Steps 3–5 on page 24.) Wrap all tightly together with strips of masking tape.

3. Drill hanger holes with ⁵⁄₆₄" bit. Install #5 skip-tooth blade and cut out crosses with saw set at medium speed (see picture below). The brass will slow down cutting speed.

Continued on page 96

Above, finished project size: 1½" x 2⅜". Various finishes.

Continued from page 94

4. Using rag or paintbrush, finish wooden crosses with stain, paint, or natural Danish oil finish. (Refer to Project Finishing on page 19.)

5. Brass cross can be left natural or polished with fine sandpaper. Either way, the brass will eventually tarnish to a nice patina when exposed to the light and air.

    NOTE: Scroll saws are also used to cut Corian, alabaster, coins, jewelry, leather, rubber, plastic, hammer handles, ball bats, boat paddles, etc.

Above, notepads, stationery, and envelopes may be dressed up by cutting a design through them with the scroll saw using a #2 skip-tooth blade. Sandwich the paper between a couple of sheets of thin plywood. Adhere Stationary Patterns found on page 97 to the top of the stack, and wrap all tightly together with strips of masking tape.

Above, Dove and heart are made from acrylic plastic Plexiglas. Use white translucent for dove and red transparent for the heart. Plexiglas is shipped with a protective film layer. Adhere patterns to protective film with spray adhesive. Use ⅛" bit to drill a hole for the dove's eye. Use ¹⁄₁₆" bit to drill hanging holes. Cut out heart with #7 skip-tooth blade, with scroll saw set at medium to slow speed. Cut out dove with #5 skip-tooth blade, at same speed. Plexiglas tends to melt back together behind blade if saw is operating at faster speeds or if smaller blades are used. (Additionally, cover top of pattern with clear packaging tape, to help cool and lubricate blade.) After cutting, remove patterns and peel-off the protective film. Clean up edges with a craft knife, if necessary.

Plexiglas Doves,
Brass Crosses, and
Paper Cutting
Patterns

13
Project

How can I make a jigsaw puzzle out of a photograph?

By adhering a photograph onto a thin piece of wood, it is easy to make a custom jigsaw puzzle.

Photo Puzzles

What you need to get started:

Tools:
- Basic tools and supplies page 13
- Scroll saw with #0 skip-tooth blade
- Photocopier
- Craft knife

Materials:
- (3) ⅛" x 4⅞" x 6⅞" Baltic birch plywood
- (3) 5" x 7" photographs

Here's how:

1. Precut all three pieces of wood to exactly 4⅞" x 6⅞". Use sandpaper to clean and smooth all edges and surfaces.
   NOTE: Wood is sized slightly under 5" x 7", because not all finished photographs are a full 5" x 7".

2. Permanently attach photograph to one piece of wood with spray adhesive by applying a liberal coat of adhesive to both back of photo and wood surface. Center photo onto wood and press into place. Lay a clean piece of paper over top of photo. Rub paper over photo firmly with fingertips, making certain every square inch is secured firmly to wood. Use craft knife to trim away any excess edges of photograph.

3. Photocopy Photo Puzzle Pattern on page 100. Temporarily adhere pattern onto wood with spray adhesive (see picture below). (Refer to Simple Fish, Steps 3–5 on page 24.)

4. Stack three layers of wood together then secure tightly with short strips of masking tape around edges. Place strip of masking tape on each outside piece of puzzle.

Continued on page 100

Above, finished project size: ⅛" x 6⅞" x 4⅞". No finish.

Continued from page 98

5. Install #0 skip-tooth blade in scroll saw. Start by cutting all the way across puzzle on each of the lines that cross the short dimension of puzzle (see picture below).

6. After cutting all of the short strips apart, wrap a strip or two of masking tape around sides to prevent them from moving during final cutting (see picture below). Lastly, saw off each individual piece, while holding steady pressure on top of stack.

NOTE: If fingers get too close to saw blade, use pencil eraser to hold puzzle pieces and keep them from slipping.

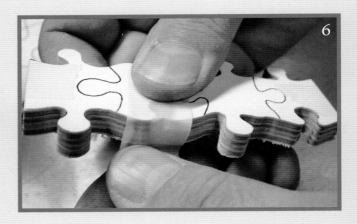

7. Remove tape and clean up edges.

Photo Puzzle Pattern

How do I make 3D objects with a scroll saw?

3D objects are no problem if you have both a front pattern and a side pattern.

3D Bunnies, Baskets, and Tulips

Here's how:

1. Photocopy 3D Bunnies, Baskets, and Tulips Patterns on page 104. Temporarily adhere patterns onto wood with spray adhesive. Position fold line on corner of wood and press pattern firmly on two adjoining sides of the wood block (see picture below). (Refer to Simple Fish, Steps 3–5 on page 24.)

2. Install #7 skip-tooth blade in scroll saw and cut out one side of pattern. Save waste pieces of material.

What you need to get started:

Tools:
- Basic tools and supplies page 13
- Photocopier
- Scroll saw with #5 reverse-tooth and #7 skip-tooth blades
- Drill with ⅛" bit
- Needle files

Materials:
- Mother 1" x 1" x 3½" pine
- Father 1" x 1" x 3⅝" pine
- Girl ¾" x ¾" x 2⅝" pine
- Boy ¾" x ¾" x 2¾" pine
- Arms ³⁄₁₆" x 1¼" x 6" pine
- Basket 1" x 1" x 2" pine
- Tulip 1" x 1" x 4" pine
- Dowel ⅛" x 3¾"
- Natural Danish oil

Above, finished project size approximately: ¾" x 1¼" x 3½". Natural Danish oil finish.

3. Fasten waste pieces back onto block by wrapping them tightly with masking tape (see picture below).

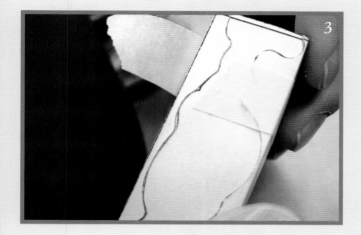

4. Flip design, and cut out remaining sections of the pattern.

5. When finished, remove all waste material to reveal project from center of wood block. Touch up any imperfections with sandpaper, needle files, etc. Finish sanding all parts to desired smoothness. (Refer to Project Finishing on page 18.)

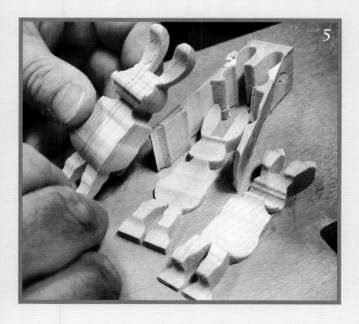

6. Cut arms for bunny family can be from ³⁄₁₆"-thick pine with #5 reverse-tooth blade. Attach arms to bodies with wood glue.

7. Repeat steps 1–5 on pages 101 and at left to make basket.

8. Begin tulip by drilling holes in bottoms of blocks for flower and leaves. Locate centers of the 1" square blocks and mark with awl. Drill ⅛" hole approximately ¼" deep into the flower block, and ⅞" deep into the leaves block (see picture below).

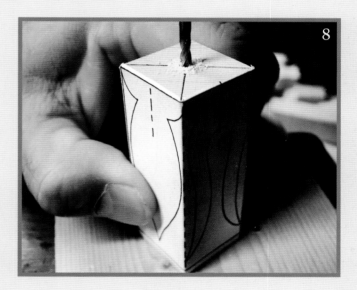

9. Repeat steps 1–5 on pages pages 101 and at left to make tulip and leaves.

10. After cutting both sections of tulip insert 3¾" length of ⅛" dowel into leaves section to serve as stem. Attach flower to top of dowel.

11. Using clean rag or foam brush, apply coat of natural Danish oil finish to all pieces. Allow to dry for a few minutes, then wipe off excess oil. (Refer to Project Finishing on page 19.)

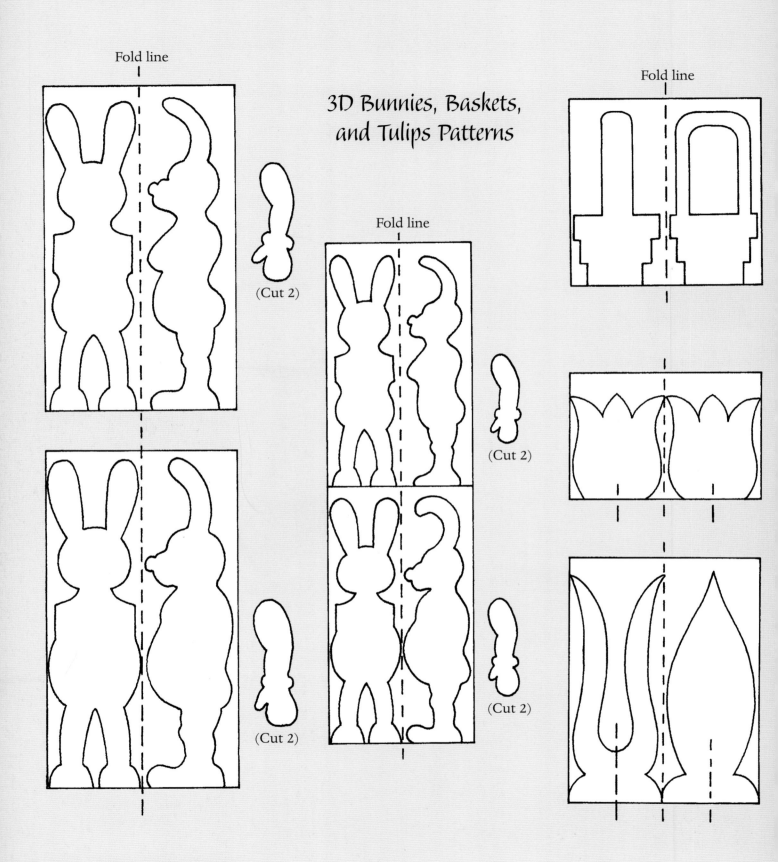

Fold line

3D Bunnies, Baskets, and Tulips Patterns

Fold line

Fold line

(Cut 2)

(Cut 2)

(Cut 2)

(Cut 2)

How do I make a basket out of a flat piece of wood?

With the use of a spiral cut, a beautiful basket can be formed from a flat piece of wood.

Collapsible Basket

Here's how:

1. Photocopy Collapsible Basket Patterns on page 104. Temporarily adhere patterns onto wood with spray adhesive. (Refer to Simple Fish, Steps 3–5 on page 24.) Cover top of pattern with clear packaging tape.

2. Extend lines from basket pattern (showing locations for screws that basket will pivot on) out to edges of wood. Transfer lines to edges of wood, and measure to center of wood (see picture below).

What you need to get started:

Tools:
- Basic tools and supplies page 13
- Photocopier
- Scroll saw with #7 reverse-tooth blade
- Drill with ⅟₁₆", ⁵⁄₃₂", and countersink bits
- Needle files
- Hammer

Materials:
- ¾" x 6½" x 9" oak
- ¾" x ¾" x 8" oak
- Packaging tape
- Natural Danish oil
- (2) #6 x 1" flathead brass screws
- (2) #6 x ¾" flathead screws

Above, finished project size: 4⅜" x 8¾" x 6⅜". Natural Danish oil finish.

3. Use awl to mark center points; then drill ⅟₁₆"
holes ¹¹⁄₁₆" deep into wood.

4. This project has been designed for ¾" thick
wood. Since actual thickness of wood varies,
often undersize, it may be necessary to slightly
alter patterns in slot areas of feet to ensure proper fit. Stand a scrap piece of wood you will be
using, on pattern in slot areas (see picture
below). If wood is thinner, or thicker, than areas
shown on patterns, trace outside of wood,
which will direct you to cut slots narrower, or
wider, as needed.

4. Locate point #1 on the pattern. Drill a ⅟₁₆" blade-
entry hole at this point (see picture below). Start
cutting here with #7 reverse-tooth blade.
Continue all the way around to separate basket
section from frame section. Then, saw around
outside of stand, and cut out feet.

5. Locate point #2 on basket area of pattern. Drill
⅟₁₆" blade-entry hole (see picture below).

6. Tilt scroll-saw work table 3° to the right (see picture below). Start cutting at point #2 and continue sawing on line as you wind your way in toward center. Stop at end of the line, and carefully remove blade from wood.

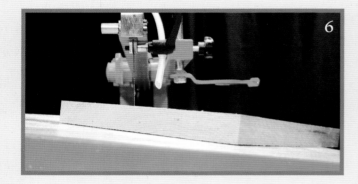

7. Lift the outer rim of the basket, carefully, as you hold down in the center. Behold the collapsing basket.

8. Remove patterns and touch up any imperfections with sandpaper, needle files, etc. Test-fit feet, and adjust slotted areas to fit. Finish sanding to desired smoothness. (Refer to Project Finishing on page 18.)

9. Use 5/32" bit to enlarge screw holes through handle section (see picture below). The screws need to turn freely in holes to allow basket to pivot. Countersink screw heads flush with outer edges. Test the fit.

10. Measure and locate center of feet joint (see picture below).

11. Use awl to mark hole location (see picture below). Drill 5/32" holes through feet. Set feet in place on bottom of stand. Insert mounting screws and gently tap them with a hammer. Remove feet and drill 1/16" pilot holes into bottom of stand to accept mounting screws.

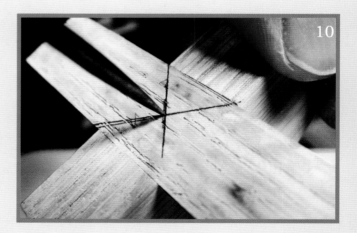

12. Using clean rag or foam brush, apply coat of natural Danish oil finish. Allow to dry for a few minutes, then wipe off excess oil. (Refer to Project Finishing on page 19.) Install #6 x 1" screws to hold basket in place inside stand, and attach feet with #6 x ¾" screws. (Remove screws and feet whenever you want to store basket.)

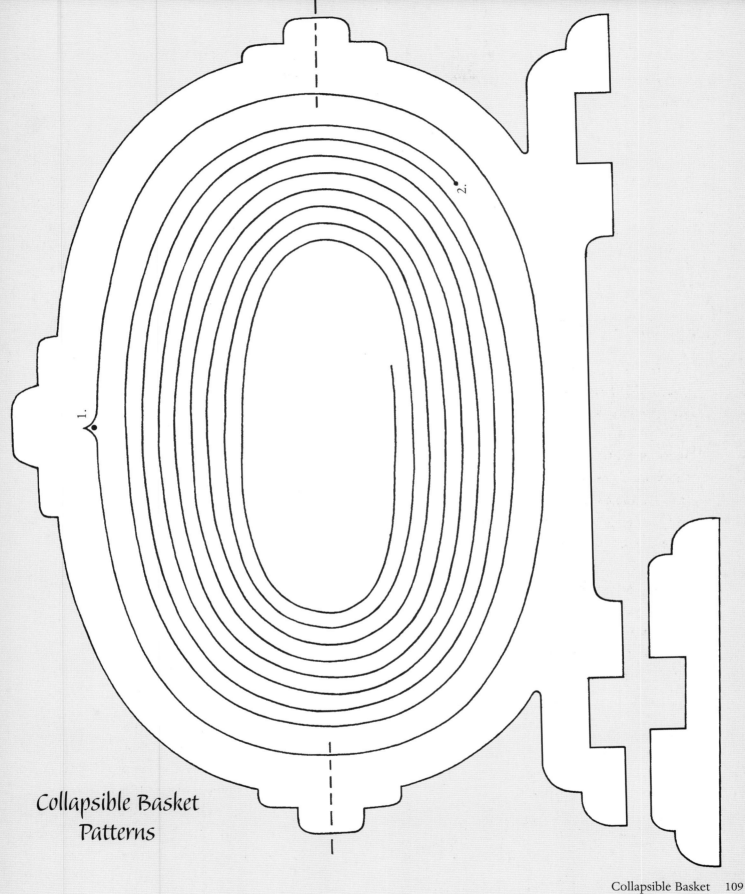

Collapsible Basket
Patterns

Acknowledgments

I wish to thank a very special group of family and friends. First, Joe Diveley, for suggesting my name to this publisher. Had circumstances been different, you would probably be holding his book in your hands. A great friend to a great many people, Joe has enthusiastically supported everything and everyone in the scroll-sawing business for many years, and greatly helped to increase the popularity of the craft. I must thank my wife, Karen, for her help sawing, sanding, finishing projects, setting up displays for photography, juggling words to help me describe it all, and much more. Many thanks to Terry Pluemer, who performed miracles with his digital photography.

I also wish to express my gratitude to James Reidle and Patrick Spielman for first introducing me to scroll-sawing, almost twenty years ago. To Carl Weckhorst whose houseful of amazing scrollsaw fretwork was an inspiration. Thanks to my good friend, Robert Becker, who is always a positive influence and has provided tremendous opportunities to showcase my talents. A special thanks to my Mom, Nita Boelman, who first put a pencil in my hand a very long time ago.

Metric Equivalency Chart

mm-millimeters cm-centimeters
inches to millimeters and centimeters

inches	mm	cm	inches	cm	inches	cm
⅛	3	0.3	9	22.9	30	76.2
¼	6	0.6	10	25.4	31	78.7
⅜	10	1.0	11	27.9	32	81.3
½	13	1.3	12	30.5	33	83.8
⅝	16	1.6	13	33.0	34	86.4
¾	19	1.9	14	35.6	35	88.9
⅞	22	2.2	15	38.1	36	91.4
1	25	2.5	16	40.6	37	94.0
1¼	32	3.2	17	43.2	38	96.5
1½	38	3.8	18	45.7	39	99.1
1¾	44	4.4	19	48.3	40	101.6
2	51	5.1	20	50.8	41	104.1
2½	64	6.4	21	53.3	42	106.7
3	76	7.6	22	55.9	43	109.2
3½	89	8.9	23	58.4	44	111.8
4	102	10.2	24	61.0	45	114.3
4½	114	11.4	25	63.5	46	116.8
5	127	12.7	26	66.0	47	119.4
6	152	15.2	27	68.6	48	121.9
7	178	17.8	28	71.1	49	124.5
8	203	20.3	29	73.7	50	127.0

About the Author

Dirk Boelman was born with a passion to draw, design, and create. There are very few days that go by when he does not have a pen or pencil in his hand.

Dirk has combined his artistic talents and woodworking skills into a full-time business that he and his wife, Karen, operate from their home in beautiful Southwest Wisconsin.

He has been referred to as "Today's most talented and productive designer and developer of fine scroll saw fretwork patterns," and dubbed "Scroll saw artist extraordinaire" by the editor of *Creative Woodworks & Crafts* magazine. Over the past 17 years, he has drawn thousands of scroll saw patterns. His work appears in books by Patrick Spielman and Jim Tolpin, and in many magazines, and other publications. He also sells and distributes his patterns through mail order catalogs, stores, and his own internet site at www.theartfactory.com.

Dirk's passion for scroll sawing goes far beyond just drawing patterns.. He has sawn hundreds of projects on a scroll saw. These items range from miniature animals smaller than a dime in size, to huge clocks standing over 9' tall.

Dirk has also experimented with sawing many different types of materials and reviewed several brands of scroll saws. He also tests other woodworking tools and related supplies.

Dirk gratefully acknowledges that he learned a great deal about woodworking and mechanics from his father and both grandfathers, who were all very skilled with their hands. Always a good listener, he was fortunate to learn many tricks of the trade from local carpenters and craftsmen. In addition, Dirk has had the opportunity to talk with scroll-saw enthusiasts from around the world.

Dirk has written numerous articles for magazines, filled with tips, techniques, instructions, and helpful advice. He has been featured in videos, has published his own quarterly newsletter, conducted numerous seminars and workshops, and attends several events across the United States each year to meet with people and talk about scroll sawing.

Index